MW01069039

"Passionate, determined, authentic, creative, thoughtful are just a few words that describe my friend of thirty-five years. I am an eyewitness of the fruit of Susan's life—the result of seeking God with all her heart, soul, and mind. Susan exhorts me to believe for the *Greater*. Be ready to be inspired and changed."

Mary Beth McElroy
Kingdom Rain International Ministries, Tulsa, OK

"This book is for Christians who spend much of their prayer time doing all the talking and none of the listening. From years of seeking to hear God's voice and a heart sold out to Him, Susan Ekhoff shares experiences from her own journey and gives readers easy to follow practices that will help them develop a more *interactive* prayer life."

LaVon Hamilton
Church of the Resurrection, Leawood, KS

"Desiring a deeper and richer prayer life, my bookshelves are filled with various methods of prayer. All conclude—it's a conversation with God, but the *how* was missing. Susan Ekhoff has captured the simplicity and relevancy of prayer. This book isn't another theory. It is the outcome of her personal experience in growing both in faith and a deeper understanding of the work of the Holy Spirit in prayer. We do have a communicating God, and He desires a dialogue with each of His children. *Prayer That Must, The Power of Conversational Prayer* will enrich your prayer life."

Anne Marie Ezzo
Co-founder of Growing Families International

Prayer
that must

Prayer
that must

THE POWER
OF
CONVERSATIONAL PRAYER

SUSAN EKHOFF

Prayer That Must, The Power of Conversational Prayer
Copyright © 2017 Susan Ekhoff

All rights reserved. No part of this book may be used or reproduced in any manner whatsoever without express written permission, except in the case of brief quotations embodied in critical articles and reviews.

Available from Amazon.com, CreateSpace.com, and other retail outlets

All scripture quotations, unless otherwise indicated, are taken from the Holy Bible, New International Version®, NIV®. Copyright ©1973, 1978, 1984, 2011 by Biblica, Inc.™ Used by permission of Zondervan. All rights reserved worldwide. www.zondervan.com. The "NIV" and "New International Version" are trademarks registered in the United States Patent and Trademark Office by Biblica, Inc.™

Scripture quotations identified AMPC are taken from the Amplified® Bible, Classic Addition, Copyright © 1954, 1958, 1962, 1964, 1965, 1987 by The Lockman Foundation . Used by permission.

Italics in scripture quotations indicate the author's added emphasis.

ISBN-13:978-1496185563
ISBN-10:1496185560

To

MY PROMISED GENERATIONS

I was honored to pray for you in advance.
The Lord is faithful.

TABLE OF CONTENTS

Part 1, Foundations of Conversational Prayer

Beautiful Exchange   17

The Anointing   33

Treasure   41

Part 2, Principles Conversational Prayer

Understanding Conversational Prayer   53

How the Lord Speaks   63

In the Midst of His Voice   71

Acting on the Lord's Voice   83

Part 3, Channels of Conversational Prayer

The Prayer That Must Know   93

The Prayer That Must Wait   101

The Prayer That Must Win   113

The Prayer That Must Be Written   129

The Prayer That Must Have Truth   141

The Prayer That Must Let Go   151

The Prayer That Must Worship   165

The Prayer That Must Be Silent   175

The Prayer That Must Leave A Legacy   187

Appendices

Who is God?   191

Erin's Second Song   197

Acknowledgements

No one writes alone, me least of all. Family and friends please read on and receive my sincere thanks for your support and encouragement.

Richard, I know Jesus more because your love reflects His. Thank you for giving and forgiving as you lived these stories beside me. Had you not supported this writing project so enthusiastically, I would never have finished. I love you better than anyone else on earth.

Benjamin, Hannah, Lydia, Mary, Samuel, Julia, and John, thank you for giving me the space to scribble away day-by-day and for praying over me when I was bogged down. This book is for you and your children's children. I have finally recorded what I needed you to know about a life of prayer, and now I ask you to live the truths shared and faithfully teach them to your children.

A heartfelt thanks to my mother, Sandra Strange, my mentor, counselor and confidant. I know about the power of conversational prayer because you modeled it for me. Thanks for patiently listening as I read the chapters of this book over the phone and for thinking each new installment was the best chapter yet—as only a *mother* could. Isn't the Lord good to bind us together as authors in this season? God's blessings on your newly published book *The Lamp, Be Aglow and Burning with the Spirit*. I am so proud of you!

To my editor Dr. Mark Hall, your brilliance and precision have safely guided this book to its final version. In the midst of a university dean's schedule, you somehow found time to speak into my book. I am so very honored and thankful.

Lydia Ekhoff, Richard Ekhoff, and Leslie Wells, your edit of the book was indispensable. Thank you for pouring over the details and offering your unique insights. I am grateful, as will be the reader!

Hannah George, thank you for helping me design the cover. Your creative genius inspires me! And no one can make Photoshop behave like you do.

My faithful "Witness" writing friends, you were my sounding board and accountability, and I am deeply indebted to you. Keep writing! I believe in you.

Karen Hardin, Susan Reidel, and Therese Stenzel, thank you for answering specific questions within the realm of your expertise as published authors. Your comments guided me over the sketchy places when I couldn't fathom the next step.

Tamara Beasler and Karli Wilson, thanks for sharing your savvy math advice.

Lord, thank You for walking me through the experiences described in these chapters—thanking You will take an eternity.

If that were not enough, You swept in with more than enough wisdom and strength to *write* the story. I will always treasure this season of wrangling with words, designing, and formatting because in the struggle, Your Spirit sustained me. I love You.

Introduction

I love visiting new places, especially those that surprise me into worship. These kinds of adventures help me know God more.

I once backpacked the Appalachian Trail. I was much younger then, and it was only a short three days, but even three days were enough to make me hate the sight of civilization. Hiking there was like taking residence in a cathedral, and the sound of the streams that crisscrossed the trail spoke to me deeply like the very voice of God. Here His majesty and peace enfolded me.

Some years later while on a mission's trip, several friends and I biked a portion of the dike that skirts Holland, with fields below on my right and the sea not quite so far below on my left. Rounding a curve, a quaint stone windmill came into view. Just beyond was a tidy Dutch village with bridges arched over narrow canals in the most inviting way. I felt that the Lord was revealing His hospitality.

I once floated the swift current of the Rhine River through the heart of Basil, Switzerland—without an inner tube. It seemed the sensible thing to do on a blistering day after too many hours in a twelve-passenger van with my college friends. If you can believe it, the water was an unforgettable shade of turquoise. But as the scenery slipped past, a little too quickly, I began to wonder how I would break through the current and get back to shore. I did, of course, eventually. It was a delicious experience despite the risks. Here I learned first-hand that adventures with God have a risk factor.

Many years later, on a half-day excursion accompanying an Alaskan cruise, my group canoed with a guide across a remote lake. At my request, she lifted a manageable chunk of glacier ice floating past and placed it in my hand. Turning it slowly, I watched the dim sunlight shimmer on the surface of its faces and pondered its surprising weight and density. Ancient snowstorms had formed the masterpiece I held in my hands. Unfathomable. Then I understood a little better that our God is called the Ancient of Days for good reason.

Once, on a two-day layover in route to China, my small group stood mesmerized on "The Peak" overlooking Hong Kong at sunset. The sight of layer upon layer of skyscrapers, each unique in color and design, stretching to Victoria Harbour, then out again to the mountain-crested horizon far, far beyond, left me dizzy and a bit shaken. I never knew before that moment that a horizon could be so wide and deep. That view gave me a glimpse of the magnitude of the love of God for vast multitudes of people.

Adventures like these are thrilling. Their breadth and beauty, facets and surprises, welcome and wonder increase my understanding of God and teach me to love Him. But the highest adventure of my life hasn't been visiting an awe-inspiring place. It has been a simple running conversation with Jesus spread over the routine days of my life. I have found that His voice is the launching place to all worthy destinations. Knowing Him is having every adventure.

In the following chapters, I share some of these personal journeys in prayer. Part One is the story of how Jesus drew my family and me to Himself—I stand in awe! In Part Two, we look intently at the voice of God—how personal and intentional is His reaching love. And in Part Three, I describe nine specific ways He has shown me His kindness, wisdom, and direction through prayer. Although these avenues of prayer are described in categories for understanding and application, in truth, a cry from our hearts never needs to be dissected. Our attentive Father eagerly responds to our need to know Him. His answers to our prayers reveal Love.

I would like to add that this book is not intended to be a scholarly treatise on the discipline of prayer. I'm drawing a distinction between the discipline of prayer and the easy conversation that flows from a relationship with The One we love. This book is mostly my personal testimony and subsequent teaching on the joys of a lifestyle of prayer.

Thank you for joining me as I share my best adventure. May the true stories on the following pages showcase the persistence of the Father's love, and may the end of the matter be this: Each of us *must pray.*

Lord, help me glorify You.
Susan Ekhoff, 5/17

PART ONE

Foundations of Conversational Prayer

The old has gone; behold, the new is here!
2 Cor. 5:17

Beautiful Exchange

In the past God spoke to our ancestors through the prophets at many times
and in various ways, but in these last days he has spoken to us by his Son . . .
Heb. 1:1–2a

The year 1967 was a kairos year for my family, and we still marvel over it. That year God broke in and did miracles. And none of us have been the same.

At that time my father Bill Worley had been an alcoholic for most of his adult life. Dad wasn't violent or abusive when intoxicated—I've thanked God for that mercy. When he was sober, Dad was kind and gentle. When he was drunk, he was passed out. In my earliest memories he is stretched across the sofa in the den. Sometimes he spent an evening with the family, but he was mostly absent from my life as a little girl.

Somehow he managed to keep his job as an accountant for a local firm in our hometown Danville, Virginia. My mom Sandra shouldered everything else. She was so self-sacrificing that my sister and I, three and six respectively, didn't know that our home was different than anyone else's.

I sensed the conflict between my parents but little understood the misery they both endured. There was the Christmas I had asked for a red bike. It was purchased ahead and stored at my aunt's home a half block away, awaiting the big day. Dad had agreed to fetch the bike as soon as my sister and I were tucked in bed Christmas Eve. But when Mom came downstairs to give the "all's clear," Dad was in a stupor, past waking. The evening was bitter and icy, but she'd just have to go herself. As she backed down the steep drive the wheels lost traction and she skidded into the mailbox across the street. Bless her, the bicycle was eventually placed beside the Christmas tree. I fondly remember that on the first fair day, Dad taught me to ride that bike in our backyard, but his companionship was a rare treat.

Dad's addiction and Mom's desperation were discretely concealed from friends and family. When Mom gave up and packed to leave, she always unpacked again. She never believed that divorce was a moral option. In his written testimony Dad recounts life as a slave to alcohol:

> My daily alcohol necessity was three pints. This much I had to have just to function, what I had come to believe was normal. Over and above that, I was a very heavy social drinker. I drank as much beer, wine, and whiskey as anyone I knew.
>
> My three pints were always consumed in secret. It was no longer a secret to my wife—had not been for a long time. She could easily find my favorite hiding spots. Even so, she knew nothing to do that might prove beneficial to me. If she poured it out, I would get more, if I did not have two more bottles already stashed nearby. If she diluted the alcohol with water, I could instantly tell. There was no way to trick me into consuming less. My body had come to need those three pints. Three pints it had to be, or I would soon be racked with nervous trembling.
>
> My days began with an immediate trip to the bathroom where with trembling fingers, I poured the first of the daily dosage of liquid fire into my often gagging and retching throat. Sometimes, too often, it came back, but I would quickly follow it with another. Later, after a second or third straight shot, I could brush my teeth and begin getting dressed.
>
> Lunch hours were spent driving my car around lonely country roads as I sipped long draughts from a bottle then chased the alcohol with a bottle of soft drink.
>
> When evening came, I went home for the day, or to dinner should night work be required. (It frequently did.)
>
> My immediate arrival was always preceded by a lengthy drive in the country for the same purpose. I remember

thinking as I enjoyed the serenity and beauty of the countryside, how dull and dreary it must be without the pulse quickening liquid I drank. Little did I know my eyes were clouded and my senses dulled by the alcohol I credited with such excellent qualities.

Be Holy

Enter Jesus. January of 1967 Mom heard a sermon that changed her life. The pastor of her Methodist church preached on "A Life of Holiness," a daily appointment with God for expressing concerns, listening for answers, reading scripture, and singing a hymn. Finally, here was something she could do! Hope surfaced for the first time in ever so long. She later said of that bright morning, "If anyone had offered to grant me a wish, I would have asked for holiness. Even more than financial freedom, a better marriage or help for Bill's alcoholism, I desired holiness." Here is Mom's first-hand account of the first months of her quest for holiness:

> I set aside 10:00 a.m. as God's time. Susan was in kindergarten, and Sandra, three years old, was usually happily at play at that time.
>
> I opened my Bible to Genesis 1:1 and began to read. Then I read some Psalms, then lots from Proverbs. I liked the book of Proverbs. I could identify with them. The Old Testament comforted me.
>
> Bible reading finished, I then began to pray. "Dear God, make Bill stop drinking. I can't stand him the way he is." I poured out all my loneliness and all our other problems, which were numerous.
>
> Then I sat there listening—wondering most of the time what it was like for God to speak to you and what I would do if He did. God's time completed, I went about the rest of the day.
>
> I went through this same routine, some scripture and some prayer, from January until April.

This time alone with the Lord became Mom's lifeline. Her search for God had begun, or shall I say, the Great Shepherd of the sheep was determined to find her.

Revival

One Monday morning in May, my mom opened the newspaper to find a full-page article about a citywide revival. It appeared the opening service at Neil's Tobacco Warehouse in downtown Danville had been quite the success. As many area churches were sponsoring the event, hundreds of people had attended. Curious about the general excitement, Dad and Mom decided to attend Monday night. Dad, unimpressed, stayed home with us girls the next two evenings. Undaunted, Mom went on to the revival without him.

On Wednesday night the guest evangelist Dr. Philpot shared his testimony. He claimed to have been healed of alcoholism. Mom was a nurse and knew that alcoholism has no medical cure. Could God really save and heal an alcoholic?

By Saturday Mom knew enough of revival protocol and vocabulary to value altar calls. Obviously, what Dad needed was to be "saved," so she conspired to give him the opportunity for this life-changing experience. The plan was as follows: My Grandmother Worley would watch my sister and me for the evening, and Mom would somehow get Dad sobered and to the revival service. At the invitation for salvation, she would go to the altar in hopes that he would follow and be changed—perhaps even healed.

The "emotionalism" involved in this type of behavior was not part of her upbringing. She had never been to an altar for anything except communion, confirmation, and once to pray for her mother, but she was willing to submit to the process for Dad's sake. In her mind, people who were raised in church were already Christians. She would simply "rededicate" her life.

With dad's sister Mary Abbott as her accomplice, she was able to get Dad sobered with tomato juice and coffee and loaded into the car in time for the Saturday night service. As the three of them set out for downtown, they each lit up a cigarette. They were on their way to the revival! I'll let her tell you what happened that night.

> I have no idea what Dr. Philpot preached on that Saturday night. I was waiting for the altar call. As soon as it was given, I moved right out. I arrived at the altar first.

I was standing there all wrapped up in self-righteousness and hoping Bill would come, when quite suddenly, I was aware of the presence of the Lord and was convicted of my *own* sins! I really thought I was going to faint. One thing I knew for sure was that I was an unrepentant sinner. I asked forgiveness for my sins and asked Jesus to come into my life.

Immediately, I was immersed in the love of God! It started at the top of my head and went to the ends of my toes. I was literally washed in love. I stood there knowing that in this moment I was without sin. I knew I had been born again. I knew Jesus as Savior and Lord. I was aware of the Holy Spirit as a workable force in my life.

To this day I don't know how I just stood there. I wanted to shout and leap for joy! Pieces of scripture flowed through my mind: "joy unspeakable" (1 Pet. 1:8), "peace that passes all understanding" (Phil. 4:7), "He went walking and leaping and praising God" (Acts 3:8) came into my thoughts, but I dared not! Yes, the joy and peace were overwhelming.

Then I heard Dr. Philpot telling all those that had come to the altar to go back into the prayer room. As I looked around, I was amazed at the number of people who had responded by coming forward—and right behind me was Bill.

We went into the prayer room, and the counselors were working with everyone. How wonderful it was when I was asked, "Do you accept Jesus as your Savior?" I answered with everything that was in me, "Yes!" I had never been so happy. I was given a little red Bible with scriptures for salvation and a page to fill in the date of commitment. May 6, 1967 became a very special date.

I went over to Bill. Two counselors were working with him. He readily confessed his sins. He was at least aware he was a sinner. All would go well until one of them would ask him if he wanted to accept Jesus as his Savior. He would say, "I've got to think about that." So it went for forty-five minutes until finally everyone gave up.

The three of us, Mary, Bill and I returned to the car. They lit up cigarettes, and I sat there with absolutely no desire for one.

The next morning I awakened with all the love, peace, and joy with which I had gone to bed. I looked out of our bedroom window at the most beautiful Sunday morning I had ever seen. I was tuned into nature. As I looked at our lawn, I saw each blade of grass. I saw each leaf on the tree, each different, and yet the same. I heard many birds singing, and yet I could hear each individually. They were all glorifying God. The grass was the greenest green, the sky, ever so blue. All of nature was sharp and alive with the glory of God.

I sat down from habit with my Bible and opened to the New Testament. Then miracle of miracles—Jesus was alive in the pages!

Give Thanks

My mom was a new creation. It was impossible for Dad not to notice. He curiously observed while she consumed the Word, frequented Bible studies, and developed Christian friends. As the weeks passed his spiritual hunger began to rise.

One day mid-June, during her Bible reading and conversation with Jesus, Mom came to this passage from 1 Thess. 5:18, "give thanks in all circumstances, for this is God's will for you in Christ Jesus." The printed words seemed to leap off the page and sparkle. She discerned that Jesus wanted her to apply these very words as an act of her will and faith. She knew that something that seemed bad was about to happen, but she should praise God anyway.

A few hours later the "all circumstances" materialized. My father's boss phoned to say he had fired Dad, who'd been seated like a zombie at his desk all morning. He was genuinely concerned, guessing that drugs were involved. He was right—Dad had added tranquilizers to his three pints of alcohol that morning.

This was the worst possible news because Mom's private-duty nursing position had just ended, which meant no income at all. But hadn't the Lord said to rejoice no matter what? "Choosing joy" became the overall characterization of the rest of her life.

Healed

It happened that the following day our family had been invited to visit friends in the Shenandoah Valley of Virginia, several hours away. Dad had never fully sobered from the day before and didn't even know he'd lost his job. Mom helped him into the backseat where he slept most of the trip.

Later that afternoon she encouraged him to consider reading a book she'd just received from one of her new Christian friends, *Beyond Ourselves*, by Katherine Marshall.[1] In the first five pages Marshall had expertly addressed some of Dad's questions about a personal God. "Just read the first few pages," she encouraged.

As Dad read, faith was birthed and Deism (the belief that God created the universe, wound it up, and then stepped away to let it run on its own) began to lose its deceptive grip on his intellect. He devoured the entire book that same night.

On Sunday morning, Dad challenged God to personally reveal Himself in a specific way: He had a cyst on his lower eyelid that he could see in his line of vision. It had become a real irritation. He'd sought medical help but had been told that the cyst was too dangerously close to his eye to be surgically removed. Standing before the bathroom mirror, Dad prayed his first prayer in years, "God, if You care anything about me, remove this growth from my eye." And God heard.

Back in Danville early Monday morning, Dad sheepishly entered the kitchen. Mom was preparing breakfast. "Do you notice anything different about me?" he questioned. She could see nothing different at all. "Look!" he said, "The cyst is gone!" Could there be any further doubt that a loving God cared about Bill Worley?

Later that night Dad risked the prayer closest to his heart, "Jesus, take away my desire to drink."

Wednesday morning the breakfast scene was repeated. Mom was seated at the table reading the paper when Dad appeared in the doorway. "Do you notice anything different about me?" She certainly noticed that he was beaming, but nothing more. Then he announced the miraculous truth. He had wakened that morning with no desire for alcohol and assured my incredulous mother that he would never drink again—he never did. He was completely healed.

In his formal written testimony, the opening paragraph reads, "I was an alcoholic. Yes, I said I *was*, not *am* . . . I am convinced that God is as alive and active here on this earth right now, as He has ever has been at any time in the history of man."

Slipping to the cemetery near our home, Dad knelt at his father's grave and submitted his life to his *personal* Savior, Healer, and Friend.

The next year he composed two poems about the Answer to his search.

Lost and Found

I rent my garb of inner-self,
Tore at my mental hair;
All of my life I'd searched for God,
But missed Him everywhere.
I sought Him in the church, at home—
Elsewhere along the way.
Each place I looked, He'd been and gone;
My thoughts turned to dismay.

Dismayed, but sure He could be found,
I went back to my task.
Someone must know just where He dwells;
But who? Who could I ask?

And then one day I chanced to think;
My search had been all wrong.
I'd looked for something tied to space;
I'd sought Him in the throng.

For God can know no bounds or ties;
He has no home as such.
He dwells somewhere beyond the skies;
He dwells in each of us.

Paradise Found

The chill that races up my spine
When wondrous chords are struck,
Is God's own hand upon my back;
A tune, His fingers pluck.

His gentle laugh is heard at length
In gurgles of a brook;
His happy thoughts are shared with me
In joy found in a book.

His fresh, sweet breath blows 'cross my cheek
In breeze of summer night.
The twinkle in His eyes shines forth
In each star's blinking light.

The snowflakes that so gently fall,
Upon my upturned face,
Are tears of joy God shed for me—
A servant of His grace.

B. A. Worley, November 5, 1968

In less than a week, my father had been healed and saved. It was time to pray about next steps. Dad had never loved accounting, but neither had he dreamed of getting the chance to do anything else. Now God called him to explore his new faith by returning to school. By fall he was a student at Candler School of Theology, Emory University in Atlanta, and my mother had a nursing position at Emory Hospital. Nothing is impossible with God.

I didn't know the details of my parents' conversions for many years, but I *felt* the transformation. I still remember the exciting seven-hour move from Danville to Atlanta, wondering aloud about the language of the people who lived in that far away place. (Atlanta might as well have been India for all I knew. I was every bit a small town girl.) My smiling mom assured me that Georgians spoke English too.

Atlanta

For the next five years mom supported the family, working all three shifts at the hospital, while my dad tackled seminary classes with their mounds of reading and research papers. He arranged his classes so that he could be home with my sister and me when Mom was at work. In these years I came to love this Dad I'd never known. He liked to play games and was a good listener. He taught me to play chess and became my trusted confidant. These were sweet, grounding years of family life, the sweetest that I had ever known, and I still treasure them.

During this Atlanta season, my parents were impacted by a move of the Holy Spirit known today as the Charismatic Movement. The Holy Spirit taught them through experience and personal study about Himself—His fruit, His gifts, His power. Once again the Lord set a precedent for the rest of our lives.

Daddy graduated from seminary in May of 1971 with his Masters of Divinity degree, but didn't necessarily feel called to preach. He and mom believed that they would possibly oversee a ministry for recovering alcoholics. As they waited for the Lord's guidance, they discussed contacting the Virginia Conference of the United Methodist Church at the first of the year.

Unexpectedly in early January 1972, Dad was admitted to Emory Hospital with a blood clot in his left arm. The diagnosis was infectious endocarditis, a rare bacterial blood infection that settles in the heart, damaging the valves and producing blood clots that can be fatal. In Dad's case the infection was traced back to dental work performed the preceding week.

My sister and I didn't understand the extent of his illness. Probably no one did. Each evening my mother, sister and I eagerly visited the hospital and shared the news of the day. As a treat, my parents allowed my sister and me to take the elevator all by ourselves to peer into the newborn nursery window. I was crazy, crazy for newborn babies. (See the chapter "The Prayer That Must Know.") Then we returned to Daddy's room to kiss him goodnight before heading back to the lonely apartment without him.

At this time of crisis for us all, God, in His grace, provided a word of knowledge. In the middle of the night, Dad awakened suddenly with the realization that he would soon die. Reaching for his Bible, it fell open to 1 Kings 20:1, "In those days Hezekiah became ill and was at the point of death. The prophet Isaiah son of Amos went to him and said, 'This is what the LORD says: Put your house in order, because you are going to die; you will not recover.'"

My mother rejected the forewarning. With the spiritual gift of faith, she resolutely believed for a complete healing. Hadn't the Lord healed Dad before? But Dad *knew* God had spoken and rested in peace beyond understanding. Obviously, this prophecy wasn't shared with my sister and me, who were elementary school age. They held it between the two of them and waited.

Pale, thin and weak, Dad returned home the first of February. He was consistent with his antibiotic medication, diet, and exercise regime, but he also resolutely put his "house in order." He instructed Mom concerning their legal documents and encouraged her to build a house. When Mom asked if they might visit Danville for Easter, he responded, "Let's not waste the time we have left." He kept the weeks uncluttered to better enjoy the joys of each day.

One morning in mid-February, Dad offered to walk us the short distance to school. He was so breathless before we had reached even the midpoint that he half collapsed on the path to rest. Seeing our frightened faces, he urged us to continue without him, overriding our anxious questions by assuring us that he was okay. He wasn't, but he eventually made it home where he confessed to Mom, "I thought I was going to die right there on the path."

One memory hurts me still. Just two nights before his death, as Dad was leaving my bedroom after goodnight kisses, I called, "Goodbye!" Oh, my, what had I said? I'd meant to say "good*night*."

Immediately, he turned back. "Why did you say that?" In my confusion, I thought up what I hoped was a reasonable explanation. "When you were in the hospital we said *goodbye* at night." I sensed he was alarmed, and I wanted to say anything that would take that look off his face. Looking back, I believe God was preparing me for Dad's departure.

Ashes

On the morning of March 8, 1972, after my sister and I had left for school, my mother entered the bedroom to find my Dad struggling to breathe. Mom administered resuscitation, but Dad left for Heaven before further help could arrive.

In that helpless moment, alone and unable to revive him, my mother glanced toward the window where the morning sunlight streamed into the room. In her spirit she realized that Dad was departing in that beam of light, but she didn't wish him back. She knew that he wouldn't want to return from the glories of Heaven, so she simply released him. As she let go, a firm assurance of God's peace enfolded her.

After His funeral in Danville, our family of three finished out the school year in Atlanta, then moved back to Danville to be near extended family. All of the rest of my growing-up years were spent in this dear place, surrounded by the people I loved most. Though we returned home in ashes, the Lord provided "the oil of joy for mourning" (Isa. 61:3). In time the Lord taught me to know Him as Father.

For my mother's complete testimony of these experiences and a lifetime of walking with the Lord, see her book *The Lamp, Be Aglow and Burning with the Spirit*, by Sandra Strange.[2]

Following Jesus for Myself

I joined my parents in The Faith in late summer of 1972, just a few months after my father's death. Mom advised that since I was now eleven, it was time to consider receiving Jesus as my personal Savior. It was an idea I'd never considered, but felt was the right decision to make.

It happened that we were attending a weeklong revival in the little country church where my parents had been married. On Thursday night when the altar call was given, I went forward mostly out of obedience to my mother, little understanding what "accepting Jesus as my Savior" meant.

I walked decisively down the creaky, wooden center aisle and knelt on the red velour altar cushion. The guest evangelist, a kind man named Jim Maharaj (from the island of Trinidad of all places), knelt facing me on the other side of the altar rail.

He asked me a series of questions. "Do you repent of your sins?"

I didn't really know what sins I might have committed, but as I paused and thought about the question, I suddenly felt an inward conviction that he was right. I was a sinner. I was truly sorry about that, so I answered simply, "Yes."

"Do you accept the free gift of salvation provided by the death of Jesus on the cross and the shedding of His blood?"

"Yes."

"Do you want Jesus to come into your life?"

"Yes."

I repeated a prayer after him phrase by phrase asking Jesus to forgive my sins and take my life as His own. And that was it. The beautiful exchange was made.

I returned to my seat—but everything had changed. I remember leaving the church that summer evening feeling light and new. The trees looked greener and the sky bluer as we made the short trip in the car down the hill to my Grandmother's home. I was already sensing that my whole life was transformed. A part of me that had previously been unstirred had now awakened in a single moment. I've never been sorry that I had made that decision.

My dad, mom, and I were three completely different people, but we equally needed a Savior. Dad had intellectual questions and an addiction that he was powerless to change. He didn't believe that it was possible to have a personal relationship with God. My mom wondered about how to be holy and how to save her marriage. Because she was a "good girl" raised in the church, she assumed that she already had a relationship with God. I was an insecure child missing my daddy and needing a Father. The Lord knew each of us intimately and was willing to meet us as individuals, exactly as we were. Jesus pursued us until we knew Him for ourselves. How I love Him for that.

Pause with me and consider God's initiative in the preceding narrative:

- A sermon on "holiness"—His idea, His power
- An evangelist who had been healed of alcoholism sharing that testimony in a warehouse revival, not ten minutes from my parent's home—His idea, His power
- A forewarning to receive bad news with joy and the faith to do it—His idea, His power
- An invitation for a weekend in the Shenandoah Valley and the gift of a book—His idea, His power
- The faith to ask for healing and receive it—His idea, His power
- The strength and peace to release a husband in death—His idea, His power
- A mother's suggestion to consider receiving Jesus as personal Savior and a daughter's obedience to follow that leading—His idea, His power

Accepting who Jesus is and what He has done for you and me is the foundation of the book that follows. Great good news! He has already initiated a relationship with each of us.

The Exchange, A Letter from Jesus

My dear child,

I have waited a long time for you to decide what to do about Me (2 Pet. 3:9, 15). If you want Me, I will come to you. If you don't, I'll wait. You are worth the wait (Rev. 3:20). I have chosen you (Isa. 43:1). I will never give up on you (Heb. 13:5–6).

I'm grieved that the relationship I desire to have with you has been so poorly explained and represented. Things that have made you fiery mad about Christianity and the Church make Me even angrier (Luke. 11:46). The things that have made you feel afraid of choosing a relationship with Me have deeply grieved Me. I ask you to forgive those who have misrepresented Me.

The truth is I wanted a relationship with you so much that I died on your behalf so that I could offer it to you now. I knew you could never earn it on your own, so I earned it for you many years before you were born (Eph. 2:8, John 14:6, Rom. 3:24, 2 Cor. 5:15). I thought of you as I died in your place so that you could have a relationship with Me. I now offer you the forgiveness of every sin. Every—single—sin. I'm listening. I care deeply.

I proved my willingness to give you new life when I died for you, but that was only the beginning (Rom. 5:6–8). I will also gift you with My friendship (Rom. 6:23, John 15:13, Prov. 18:24). You can't imagine all that I have planned for you (Rom. 8:32).

The decision to follow Me has nothing to do with an altar call. It has nothing to do with a certain church. It is not a certain prayer or place. It is simply this: You give Me all your life, and I will give you all of Mine in exchange. (John 3:3, Rom. 10:9–10, John 3:16).

If you decide to take Me up on this relationship, I give you permission to make the exchange anywhere you choose: in your favorite chair, lying on your bed, under a tree, kneeling, running. The place and time are *your* choice. At the point of exchange, I will take all of your life. Over time I will make it everything you always wanted it to be and more: a life that makes a difference, a life that blesses people, a life that leaves a legacy (Eph. 2:10, Jer. 29:11–14).

Understand that I will expect you to follow Me because your life will be Mine (John 15:14), but you never have to be afraid because I will lead you in ways that bless you, and I will provide the strength and desire to walk with me (John 10:27). As we travel together, I will teach you to love Me.

Those who know Me well will tell you that I am the kindest person they've ever known, and that they've never regretted making the exchange (Eph. 2:6–7, Jer. 9:24).

I love you. I'm waiting. Call to me. Don't wait too long.

Your truest Friend and Savior,

Jesus

* See Appendix One, "Who is God?" for a biblical perspective of Father God, Jesus, and the Holy Spirit.

Going Deeper
Questions for Small Group Discussion

1. Living with an addiction is heartbreaking and depleting. Are you struggling with an addiction or the addiction of someone you love? Is there anyone who knows the whole truth? Do you have a trustworthy confidant who will pray and listen? If not, who could you contact for support?

2. Have you ever pursued holiness? How could you make this pursuit a priority?

3. What is your worldview? Who is God? How involved is He in His creation—specifically with mankind? What is His character? What is the nature of man? Is mankind inherently good or evil? Are you willing to allow the God of the Bible to reveal the answers to these questions?

4. When a crisis comes, do you choose to rejoice? When have you seen God change a problem into a blessing?

5. Have you experienced a miracle or healing? What is the miracle you need right now in your life, or the life of someone you love? What is your specific prayer?

6. Have you lost a loved one? How did God prepare you for that loss? How has God comforted you since that time? Recommended reading in the midst of grief: Rebecca Springer's *Within Heaven's Gates.*[3]

7. To which of the three testimonies shared in this chapter do you relate the most: Bill's, Sandra's or Susan's? Has God pursued you personally? In what ways?

8. Have you made the "beautiful exchange"? If so, when did you make this most important of all decisions? If not, are you ready to make it now?

The Anointing

And we all, who with unveiled faces contemplate the Lord's glory,
are being transformed into his image with ever-increasing glory,
which comes from the Lord, who is the Spirit.

2 Cor. 3:18

The Charismatic Movement, a spiritual renewal of the late 60's and early 70's—continued to sweep through the Church bringing revival. By the fall of 1973, my mom began to hear about a weekly fellowship on Danville's North Main Street where "things were happening." It was where revival was in progress, so, of course, we went! My mom was that type of Christian. With the spiritual gift of faith, she was often one of the first to lift the cup of "new wine" to her lips. The fresh "wind" of the Spirit was attractive, even irresistible to her (Mark. 2:21–22, Acts 2:1–2).

Because the meeting place was the floor above a local business, it was called "The Upper Room" (Acts 1:12–14). Parking along the street curb and climbing the interior stairs, we entered a large, dimly lit room. The youngish worshippers seated cross-legged on the floor were singing choruses led by a guitarist. That was different. My Christian experience had been linked to pews, hymns, and organs—only. There was something very intimate about the worship. I watched and listened with interest.

Someone preached a message, but what I remember was the invitation at the end. The speaker shared that the Holy Spirit is the power of God and that at our invitation, He will fill us. He called it asking for the "Baptism of the Holy Spirit." I instinctively knew I wanted the Holy Spirit. Quietly, in my heart, I gave my assent, "Please come in. I want *all* of You."

The year before, when I repented of my sins, gave Jesus my life, and took His in exchange, I felt different immediately. When I said, "Yes" to His Spirit in this second experience, I didn't feel different at all—not at first. I was concerned about that, but I needn't have been. The relationship gently unfolded. The Lord, who is the Spirit (2 Cor. 3:18), taught me to love Him gradually over months and years. Looking back, I can see that my "yes" embraced everything the Holy Spirit wanted to give me from that day on.

Now there may be those of you who would like to close this book right here. I know that the phrase "Baptism of the Holy Spirit," or "second experience" messes with some theology. I understand why you might be offended and don't necessarily disagree with you. I'm certainly not trying to say that I didn't receive the Holy Spirit at my salvation. In this testimony my heart is to describe the beginning of a *relationship,* not the proper way to label the experience. Please feel free to say, "no," to the terminology, but wait to pass judgment on the value of a relationship with the Holy Spirit, in case the Lord has led you to our moments together. The Church has many faults, but one of our most toxic ones is tripping over terms that cause divisions. When we trip (and we will), can you and I agree between us to fall *forward?*

Growing in the Gifts of the Spirit

Following my introduction to the Holy Spirit and into my teen years, my best growth happened in Women's Aglow Fellowship (now *Aglow International,* aglow.org), established in our area in 1974. The monthly meetings featured praise and worship, a dynamic keynote speaker, and impactful prayer ministry. My mother was on the first board for the Chatham, Virginia Chapter, so I didn't miss—but I wouldn't have wanted to. I relished the monthly outreach meetings and area retreats; The Lord used them to launch my spiritual gifts and establish a fascination for the leading edge of the Spirit's movement in His Church. I was a member of *Aglow* chapters for many years and still attend their national or international conferences when able.

What I heard and saw in *Aglow* drove me to the Word. I meditated on the gifts of the Spirit (1 Cor. 12, Rom. 12) and read and reread the book of Acts to compare my understanding of His personality and activity with my own experience. I learned that every Christian receives spiritual gifts with which to glorify God and bless others. I had already received the gift of speaking in tongues at age fifteen or so and loved praying in this way for people and situations. After reading about Solomon's request in 1 Kings 3:10–15, I also asked for the gifts of wisdom and discernment.

Along with *Aglow*, I benefitted from a formal Christian education. My mom, a single parent with a slender budget, sacrificed to send my sister and me to a small Christian school in Danville for our junior and senior high school years (1974–79). The faculty and student body were the finest of any, and I deeply appreciated their influence in my life. My graduating class of just twenty-two and my high school teachers are still dear to me, even after all these years. They grounded me in ways that have lasted.

The theology of this school was staunchly Southern Baptist. Father and Son were deeply loved, but any mention of the Holy Spirit, especially His operable gifts was discouraged. Some of my teachers believed that the gifts of the Spirit, in particular speaking in tongues and healing, had ceased in validity and practice with the deaths of the first apostles, never to return to the Church. My father's healing, my personal study, and the gifts of the Spirit already in operation in my life kept me from conforming to this line of thinking. You can imagine how difficult balancing my *Aglow* training with my Baptist-based education could be at times. I did not push my beliefs on others (not much), but neither could I deny them, which would have been to deny the Lord.

Some Christians are similarly troubled about the Holy Spirit, especially His gifts. He seems like a wild card. We don't know what He might require of us, and we don't like the idea of encouraging out of control situations. When we are afraid, we may resort to lockdown mode to control the culprit of our fear. I know I do. But we can fall into error when we try to restrain the Holy Spirit. If you think about the logistics of the task, it is laughable to think we can govern the power of God. Gamaliel expressed wisdom to the Jewish Sanhedrin during the days of the early Church: "Men of Israel . . . in the present case I advise you: Leave these men alone! Let them go! For if their purpose or activity is of human origin, it will fail. But if it is from God, you will not be able to stop these men; you will only find yourselves fighting against God" (Acts 35:35, 38–39).

As high school graduation approached in June 1979, hunger for the Holy Spirit drove me to continue my education at a university where He was honored. My first and only choice was Oral Roberts University in Tulsa, Oklahoma. My mother later told me that it had been my dad's dream that I attend ORU.

God called Oral Roberts to "raise up your students to hear My voice, to go where My light is dim, where My voice is heard small, and My healing power is not known, even to the uttermost bounds of the earth. Their work will exceed yours, and in this I am well pleased." And so I was trained for four exceptional years. Amen.

I met my husband Richard on practically the first day of school our freshman year. We dated through most of college and became engaged under the Christmas tree in his parents' Tulsa home in December 1982.

Just after our graduation in the summer of 1983, Richard and I traveled with an ORU missions team to Amsterdam for a ten week "Summer of Service" with Youth with a Mission. YWAM's emphasis on friendship evangelism and the Father Heart of God changed us. The worship and intercession in a mixture of Dutch, English and French, together with missionaries of many nations opened my eyes to the beauty of the universal Church. The worship choruses we learned in Amsterdam became the music for our wedding ceremony back in Danville on September 3, 1983. This season established the worldview for our home and ministry.

After a brief honeymoon on Hatteras Island, North Carolina, we moved to Bixby, Oklahoma, so Richard could work beside his father in the family mobile home business. We were so full of excellent teaching and experience we just wanted to sink into a local congregation and serve. After a brief search, we joined First

United Methodist Church in Bixby. The family of faith that we first loved in that dear church have become lifelong friends.

The Anointing

The next chapter of life in the Spirit came in 1992 when I was thirty-one and the mother of three: Benjamin was born in 1986, followed by Hannah in 1988. Lydia joined us in 1991. By this time life had drifted into a treadmill routine. I was bored with church and discouraged in my devotional life. But in the void, spiritual hunger was rising.

Spiritual drought is often the climate for personal revival. Thus, an unexpected adventure in relational prayer was sparked when a friend shared that she had just read a book that had opened her eyes to the person of the Holy Spirit. I was intrigued by her enthusiastic description. The name of the book was *Good Morning, Holy Spirit*, by Benny Hinn.[4]

As quickly as I could get the book into my hands, I devoured every page. Here is the principle gained that changed my life and could change yours: God's people are called to have a personal relationship with the Holy Spirit. I had read about the Holy Spirit, operated in His gifts, enjoyed His presence, and produced a little of His fruit (Gal. 5:22–23), but I didn't *know Him*. How I had missed the relational part of life in the Spirit, I do not know.

When God is ready to move in our lives, revelation unfolds in days—even moments, and we can pass into places of faith and practice that were completely foreign to us before. This season was like that for me. Everything spiritual accelerated.

Ravenous desire to know the Lord became the focus of my life in those weeks. I was driven by a single, consuming goal and its procured discipline. The goal: to know the Spirit. The discipline: establishing a time and place to go deep without interruption. I determined to allow a luxurious three-hour interlude alone with the Lord before the household stirred.

Our home at that time had a detached garage connected to the house by a breezeway. I arranged a corner nook in the garage with study materials, a chair, and desk, and then set the alarm clock for 4:30 a.m.

The most grueling part of this adventure was getting up morning after morning. When the belligerent alarm announced 4:30 a.m., I barked myself a stern mental lecture about the importance of my quest until I was able to throw back the covers. When I was finally separated from the bed and balanced on my feet, I dragged myself out into the early morning and locked myself in the garage. The dreary interior was not a reward for the effort. Invariably I found myself sealed inside with a persistent mosquito. My eyes were so bleary that they barely focused. I had arrived, but what next? I had no experience to guide me further. How does one know the Spirit of the Lord anyway?

By default I began with singing because it was the best way to stay awake. After walking and worshipping awhile, I walked and prayed awhile. I prayed for revelation about a relationship with the Lord. I prayed for my family and church. When I was sufficiently awake enough to see, I opened my Bible to read and recorded impressions in a notebook, walking again when I started to doze.

It took several months, but after the testing period had been endured, I passed into the joy of the discipline. I intentionally went to bed by 9:30 p.m., or earlier if I had the treat, then leapt up at 4:30 a.m., donned a sweater, and hurried across the breezeway to my trysting place, lest I miss a moment with the Lord. A routine formed around worship, intercession, study, and writing.

The walking-singing-prayer part was braided by the Lord into a cherished time of listening and petitioning, fused with worship. I learned to depend on the Holy Spirit to reveal the thoughts and intents of the Father and pray into what He revealed. I prayed aloud in English and in tongues. Prayer took on the boldness of intercession—and the Lord answered my prayers.

When I sensed that fellowship and prayer were complete, I went to my desk and took out my study materials. After a bit of memorization of scripture, I recorded answers to prayers and studied topics of interest. I studied the ministry of the Holy Spirit, the altar of the soul, and resting in truth. Topics that "would preach" poured forth passionately, filling my notebook pages. Much of what I learned early on was compiled into a study titled "The House of God" about life in the Spirit. I was willing to sit at the feet of the Holy Spirit and He was more than willing to lead and teach.

The time came when I didn't want to return to the house at 7:30 a.m. I stood with my hand on the doorknob and prayed that the Spirit would not urge me to leave Him but would enter my day with His glory—and He did. I didn't want to keep the truths that had so thrilled me in my garage sanctuary to myself; indeed, I could not. I was thankful that the Lord provided outlets of expression. I had the joy of teaching some of what I learned in a Sunday school setting and prayed for opportunities to turn everyday conversation to the Lord. I was falling in love with the Holy Spirit and didn't care who knew.

Many spiritual disciplines are like this one. A price must be paid; some part of our flesh must die before the reward of breakthrough is granted. In the miserable initial struggle, we can be tempted to forsake the goal. But thanks be to God in this case my desire was too strong to be denied. I wanted to know the Spirit of the Lord! By His mercy I was enabled to press past my aversion for middle of the night meetings so I could experience the delight of a relationship with Him. This breakthrough was made possible by the Spirit's strong, persistent call to come away with Him and know Him for myself. He provided the desire and power to pursue that end until it was fulfilled.

All that I had learned in my past became the foundation for this fresh year and a half *away* with the Spirit of Jesus and launched what followed in my next seasons. In the aftermath I find that I am enduringly awakened to my love for Him and His love for me. I operate in an awareness of being *in* Him for "He himself gives everyone life and breath and everything else . . . In Him we live and move and have our being" (Acts 17:25b, 28a). Having broken through to genuine worship in this private, intentional way, genuine worship is now more easily attainable in public. Enjoying Him is my quintessence, the unsurpassed center of my life—the part from which all else flows.

When the Lord desires, He still calls me to be away with Him in preparation for shifting seasons, and I will be required to break through again in the very early morning discipline of fellowshipping with Him. He has proved that He is more than worth the pain of the discipline.

This fellowship with the Holy Spirit (2 Cor. 13:14), the anointing, became my preparation for better understanding and enjoying the scriptures and experiencing what I call "prayers that must," or conversational prayer, in the chapters that follow.

Going Deeper
Questions for Small Group Discussion

1. What do you know about the Holy Spirit? What is your experience with Him?

2. Have you ever experienced spiritual hunger—longed to know God more? What steps did you take to fulfill that longing? How did the Lord meet that need?

3. Where and when do you meet with the Lord? Describe the place and your time alone with Him.

4. When the Holy Spirit enters our lives, He brings His gifts (Rom. 12:4–8, 1 Cor. 12:4–11, Ephesians 4:11–13). Which gifts do you see at work in your life? Which gifts do you see in the lives of those who influence you the most?

5. Have you ever pursued a spiritual discipline? Were you eventually able to break through to a place a joy? Describe that experience.

Treasure

Heaven and earth will pass away,
but my words will never pass away.
Luke 21:33

Richard's parents Ralph and Wanda Ekhoff owned various properties over the years, but the family favorite was a ten-acre strip in south Tulsa. When it was purchased in the seventies, it was well past the civilization of Tulsa proper, banked with longhorn steers to the east and woods to the west. Christened "The Farm," it was the place where the family boarded their two horses, hosted hayrides, and raised tomatoes.

Later, in the eighties, Ralph bought a mobile home and placed it on the acreage for his aging parents. After their deaths the ten-acre strip was divided into two-and-a-half acre lots and eventually three were sold to other families, but Ralph and Wanda retained the fourth.

By this time, Tulsa had grown up around the spot, making it a country oasis in the midst of housing developments and commerce. Richard's dad periodically mentioned the possibility of our building a home on this last two-and-a-half acre lot, but we didn't really consider it. Building a house was vague and dream-like in those years.

Then in early 2002 we learned that our leased home of twenty years would be sold—not immediately, but most certainly. So, we began an earnest search for a house in our area, a house with a bit of land for a family of nine. Yes, we now had four more children: Mary was born in 1993, Samuel (1995), Julia (1997) and John (1999). The "sensational seven" were now ages three to sixteen, and our house was brim-full of spirited living and homeschool.

As you can imagine, we had a few thoughts about the kind of house we would like to have. We most definitely wanted a place to s p r e a d o u t ! But in addition, I preferred colonial architecture, a house with "good lines" and "country charm." Richard insisted on a downstairs master bedroom. I wanted a huge center island workspace in the kitchen. Richard wanted an accessible walkout attic. I wanted a utility room that had enough space for a craft table and children's lockers. We both wanted a nook that could be used as a library where favorite books that had been too long relegated to the attic could be brought out and enjoyed. Most importantly, Richard and I wanted a house where we could have a family ministry of hospitality.

Realtors drug us all over the county, but we were by no means easy to please. We kept hoping that a house befitting our needs, wants, and single income budget existed somewhere. We encouraged each other that we would know the home God was providing when we saw it. But while Richard remained characteristically optimistic, I feared the house didn't exist.

To our horror, during this full year of frustrated searching, our fifty-year-old home began falling apart in earnest. The septic system was shot. I will not describe this nasty, oozy problem except to say that commode overflows were an almost daily event. The roof leaked in many rooms making rainy nights dreadful. Not knowing if the new owner would use the existing house or bulldoze it prevented us from investing in expensive repairs. With these escalating frustrations, and no foreseeable outlet for a move, I became discouraged, then miserable. In desperation I asked the Lord to restore my hope in a specific way.

Now, each year I ask the Lord for a birthday present and my forty-second birthday, November 28, was approaching. (I share how this tradition began and other birthday stories in a later chapter "The Prayer That Must Wait.") After much prayer and discernment, I felt the Lord was inviting me to ask Him for a *glimpse* of my new home. By *glimpse* I meant an idea of what our new house might be like.

This was a "restore hope" request. I did not ask to own the home or even know for sure which one the Lord had chosen for us. I just wanted to be assured that somewhere out there was an affordable, comfortable home. Recording the formal petition in my journal on my birthday, I remember thinking that He might show me a picture in a magazine, or maybe I would drive by a house that would help vision me.

As I woke on Saturday morning, just two days later, I was at once aware of the Lord's voice. He was pressing the idea of *building* a home into my heart with conviction and creativity! I was surprised. "Really, Lord?!"

Eagerly, I gathered pencil, paper and a straight edge and began to draw a partial floor plan. As I sketched, the Lord revealed that the center of our home would be a double fireplace that divided the kitchen and family room. On the kitchen side, I would place two rocking chairs where I could sit with others, a "get acquainted," "cozy-in" nook. I actually drew an oval rug and two rocking chairs on the floor plan. And as I did, I was keenly aware that I was sketching my heart's desire—the symbol of a lifestyle of hospitality.

Within hours the Lord also spoke to Richard by naming our new home and instructing that our house should be built on the treasured Ekhoff family property in south Tulsa. It would be called "Heritage" (Ps. 16:6–8), a reminder of the godly heritage passed from Richard's parents and grandparents, and the heritage we would pass to those who came after us.

Wanda and Ralph graciously gifted us with a portion of their remaining two-and-a-half acre lot and an architect and builder were procured. As we pored over plans that next year, I redrew the floor plan on what seemed like a weekly basis, but the kitchen hearth and double fireplace remained untouched. It was the hub about which all other decisions—endless decisions— pivoted.

Groundbreaking finally came in January of 2004. The framing began soon afterward. We visited every day to clean up after the crew and look over the progress.

Then an idea, certainly inspired of the Lord, came to us. Placing a plastic cup filled with black sharpie markers, a Bible, and a note of instruction at the front entrance, we invited family and friends, who visited the site, to write scripture on the wooden framework of the house. Verses written by guests were signed and dated. As the months passed, God's Word was penned in every conceivable place: the staircase, pantry, garage, and closets. It became a game to see who had visited and what he or she had written on the beams. Before the house was drywalled, I took pictures of many of the scriptures so that we could remember their truths.

Today, as I sit comfortably in my family room typing these words, I am very aware of the promises just behind the drywall mask. The wisdom of scripture literally enfolds me.

Structure

Like the scripture written on the framework of our new house, the Word of God is the structure of our Christian life. When applied to the foundation and framework of our thinking, our actions and words become reflections of its internal presence. Jesus is the hospitable host of the central hearth of our being, inviting us to meet with Him in the context of His Word. When we open the scriptures, we host His presence. In time, His Word and Spirit conform us to His image. We are His workmanship created to do the good works described in His Word (Eph. 2:10).

Moses' injunction to the families of nations underscores the importance of a daily conversation with our Father that includes His written precepts: "Hear, O Israel: The Lord our God, the Lord is one. Love the Lord your God with all your heart and with all your soul and with all your strength. These commandments that I give you today are to be on your hearts . . . *Write them on the doorframes of your houses and on your gates*" (Deut. 6:4–9, emphasis mine). We are commanded to apply the Word of God to the structure of our routine lives, building our lives on God's character and ways.

The Holy Bible is the heritage of every Christian, our treasured "family land," God's gift to us all. This Word of Grace is able to build us up and give us an inheritance among the sanctified (Acts 20:32).

An Invitation to Love and Live the Word

I love my Bible and consider it my most valuable possession. Many of the highlighted, and underlined passages have brought revelation just when I needed them. The margins are sprinkled with pastors' and authors' names, family history, personal insights, prayers, and promises—some stained with tears. As the Spirit prompts, children's names are printed next to specific verses and dated. Sometimes just before I close the book, I kiss the page. Not because ink on rice paper is valuable, but because the wisdom experienced in the reading has taken me to a new level of relationship with God.

There are also times when I fall out of love with my Bible. I relax my zeal, ignore my study disciplines, and allow boredom to set in like mold. After a while an achy loneliness accompanies the boredom. It is the Spirit calling me to repent and return to the Lord in His Word. I can't bear life without Him for long.

- Scripture is more and more the sustenance of my Christian life and for good reason:
- An amalgamation of history, poetry, parables, proverbs, doctrine, teaching, prophecy, and covenants, the Bible displays the Lord's character and ways so that He can be known and rightfully adored. It has the power to reveal Truth.
- Scripture reveals the plan of salvation and holy living. Our faith comes from hearing the Word, and our actions follow, verifying that faith (Rom. 10:17, James 2:14–26).
- The scriptures are so masterfully designed that they speak personally to each situation in every generation.
- Scripture is the textbook of all wisdom. It validates or disqualifies every other word.
- It is the ultimate handbook for relationships.
- In addition the scriptures are the staple of conversational prayer. God uses His written revelation to share His heart with us, and we use its words to respond to our Father. As we memorize, study, pray, declare and bless with Word, we are rightly aligned with the mind of Christ.

Pause with me and meditate reverently on the magnitude of the revelation. From this perspective of rightful awe, how can we begin to fathom the treasure stored in pages of the Bible? Here are the holiest, most practical ways to love and live.

Best of all, the Holy Spirit is our teacher and friend as we open the Word. He brings us into conversation with the Author, making the written Word living and active. To close this chapter I would like to flashback to a childhood memory that illustrates the Bible's *relational* treasure.

The World from the Red Rocker

Some of my fondest childhood memories are centered around a sturdy red rocker in my Grandmother Easley's country kitchen. The short, broad rocker had been commissioned and constructed for her father, my great-grandfather Martin, for his front porch many years before. When Grandmother accented her kitchen with red, she decided to paint the rocker to match. I spent many a visit seated cross-legged in that chair, rocking and surveying, rocking and listening, rocking and internalizing the kitchen culture with delight.

From the red rocker, I could take in the whole room. Before me was the little round table with its fresh colorful cloth, encircled by four woven bottom chairs (a fifth was to the left of the doorway in case needed).

Glancing out the window over my right shoulder, I could just detect my grandfather bent amidst rows of vegetables in the ample family garden. A tobacco field and pond were beyond. In the summer, the window would be open and an inset box fan would usher fresher air into the room.

The top-loading portable dishwasher—a luxury indeed—was parked under the window beside the rocker. Grandmother didn't use it often, but after large gatherings, it was dutifully rolled to the sink and hooked up to the faucet to run its cycles. When it was not needed, it was the perfect place to set my glass of iced tea.

Sometimes there were baskets of beans from the garden to snap or peas to shell. The red rocker was the best place for this kind of work. Then I would watch with due respect and a little awe as grandmother expertly canned the fresh pickings in a pressure canner on the stove. (I was secretly terrified of this massive kettle, which might explode at any moment.)

I can see Grandmother, bustling about the cozy room as steam squeezed from beneath the lids of pots on the stovetop, and chicken fried in the electric skillet on the counter, chatting all the while. Being with people energized Grandmother. She loved me, and I knew it, and I loved her with all my heart. Sometimes there was just Grandmother and me, but as often as not, there was a kitchen full of people who circled up in the creaky chairs for leisurely conversation.

When my mother's three sisters (who were married and lived in other Virginia places) visited, the rocker was the merriest place to be. The aunts told hilarious family lore and laughed and laughed. When the younger cousins were shooed away to play outside, I lingered hoping to be allowed to remain. I often was. I would not have missed the mini-reunion around the rocking chair in the kitchen.

The kitchen phone was on the wall just inside the doorway. On holidays while the sweet potato casserole and savory dressing were browning in the oven, it would ring every little bit. Grandmother had a host of friends in that close knit community and ran affairs with her sweet and savory opinions. Lifting the receiver she would replace, "Hello," with "Merry Christmas!" or "Happy Thanksgiving!" I rocked and exulted in those telephone greetings because I knew they brought a surprised smile to the person on the receiving end of the line.

Grandmother Easley has been in Heaven for many years, but the conversations I experienced from the rocker linger and lift me. They are part of my heritage.

After our new home was built, my mother gifted me with Grandmother's red rocker—okay, I begged her for it and she relented! I placed it with a second rocker at the kitchen hearth just as I had sketched the scene years before on my forty-second birthday. Each day as I stir and slice, I face the nook where the two rockers sit side-by-side.

The red rocker is the center of my home, a comfy place for books read aloud and catching up with family and friends. I look forward to the day when I will rock my grandbabies there. Perhaps a grandson or granddaughter will rock and watch me cook while the aunts laugh and laugh. When I am not seated there, my heart is inclined to the place—anticipating.

Seated with Jesus

In the same way that taking my place in the red rocker brought me into fellowship with my grandmother and seats me near friends and family members in my own home today, opening the Bible ushers us to the best seat in the house to visit with the Lord for a while. When we are not seated with Him, His expansive heart is inclined toward us—anticipating intimate conversation.

Jesus desires to draw us into His Word where we begin to fathom the extent of His love for us and how we can love Him back. Sometimes we are alone with Him, and at other times we open the scriptures with a circle of friends. As we linger with Him and wrestle with the wisdom of His written revelation, His very thoughts and purposes are revealed.

Conversations with Jesus in the midst of the Word may have merry surprises that delight and encourage us. "I delight in your decrees; I will not neglect your word . . . Your statutes are my delight; they are my counselors" (Ps. 119:16, 24). At other times they bring us to our knees. The Word decisively divides and is a discerner of the thoughts and intents of the heart (Heb. 4:12). From the perspective of Scripture, the fresh culture of Heaven is ushered into our lives.

The "family stories" stored within the pages of Scripture, provide a mini-reunion with the saints of old. By comparing the work of the Lord in their lives with our own, we can gain valuable perspective and practical wisdom. The Scriptures are a record of our family heritage.

Those who transparently and whole-heartedly enter the Scriptures cannot remain the same—their worldview is infused with life. Jesus takes His written words and writes living words on our human hearts (2 Cor. 3:3). And as He does, we are changed from glory to glory (2 Cor. 3:18).

In Part One we have examined our relationship with our Father through Jesus, His Spirit, and His Word. In Part Two we will discuss the Lord's voice: how to recognize what He is saying and act on His instruction. Let the conversation begin.

Going Deeper
Questions for Small Group Discussion

1. Which Scriptures are foundational in your life? To which biblical person do you most relate? Why?

2. How do you study the Word most effectively? What are your favorite Bible study tools? Where is your study nook?

3. Which biblical disciplines do you use in your daily life: memorization, study, declaration, blessing, praying the Word, and living the Word? Share some examples. Which would you like to add to your disciplines?

4. Sitting with those we spiritually respect and asking wise questions can change the course of our lives. Who influences you with consistent study and application of the Word? When might you meet with that person?

5. Do you sense that Jesus sits with you in the midst of His Word? If not, ask Him to sit with you in the hearth room of your heart.

PART TWO

Principles of Conversational Prayer

Call to me and I will answer you
and tell you great and unsearchable things
you do not know.
Jer. 33:3

I call on you, my God, for you will answer me;
turn your ear to me and hear my prayer.
Ps. 17:6

Understanding Conversational Prayer

. . . He calls his own sheep by name and leads them out.
When he has brought out all his own, he goes on ahead of them,
and his sheep follow him because they know his voice . . .
My sheep listen to my voice; I know them, and they follow me.

John 10:3b, 4, 27

When our son Samuel was five months old, he became critically ill—literally overnight. During the preceding morning, all his symptoms were of the typical upper respiratory viral type. I assumed that he had a bad cold and would be fine. He was baby number five in our family. Hadn't I been equal to every infant crisis to date?

During the afternoon, Richard and I slipped away to attend the memorial service of a dear friend, leaving Samuel with his older siblings. During this celebration of a life well lived, a selected passage from Isaiah was read. I completely missed the reference but was aware of a significant truth pressing towards me. As the Word leapt toward me and resonated, I jotted two phrases on the order of worship in my lap: "carries the lambs in His arms" an' "gently leads those with young." I knew that the Lord wanted to savor this truth and I did, hugging it deliciously close. Af was an often-overwhelmed mother of five "lambs" at th' in constant need of being gently led.

Coming into the house an hour or so later, I deliberately set my purse and coat aside and reached for my Bible, eagerly opening it on the kitchen table. With the help of the index concordance, I easily found the verse in Isaiah 40:11 and read, "He tends his flock like a shepherd: He gathers the lambs in his arms and carries them close to his heart; he gently leads those that have young." Marking the verse and tucking it away among my heart's treasures, I went to the bassinette to check on Samuel. He was very restless and seemed feverish, obviously worse than when I had left for the service such a short time before.

For the rest of the day and into the night, I rocked him almost continually. If I laid him down for even a moment, he began a hoarse, pitiful cry, and I scooped him right back up. In the wee hours as his breathing became more labored and his temperature soared, I became increasingly alarmed. The moment came when I knew my baby was dying. Waking Richard and making quick arrangements for our four sleeping children, we rushed to the nearest hospital and through the sliding emergency room doors.

By this time Samuel was desperately struggling for air, and I was hysterical. A competent nurse took him from me, and I was ushered to a secluded corner to compose myself. I feigned sanity, and ten minutes later was allowed to take Samuel into my arms as he was examined. His oxygen level was at eighty percent caused by double pneumonia and Respiratory Syncytial Virus (RSV), a virus that can be deadly, especially for infants.

Within a few hours Samuel had been admitted to the hospital. While Richard headed home to check on our older children, Samuel and I were escorted by wheelchair from the emergency room to an austere pediatric patient room. It was simply furnished with the usual medical equipment, two unoccupied metal hospital cribs, a skimpy vinyl recliner, and a wooden rocker. I sank gratefully into the rocker. Cradling Samuel in one arm and holding an oxygen cup to his face with my free hand, I rocked and rocked letting the quiet and seclusion soothe away my frazzled terror. With stinging eyes closed, I relived the nightmare hours through which we had just passed.

Suddenly, I remembered—Hadn't the Lord spoken profoundly yesterday? What had He said to me? Oh, yes, yes! "He gathers the mbs in his arms and carries them close to his heart; he gently leads those that have young." Then I knew something that I had not known the moment before: The Lord was carrying Samuel and purposefully leading me. Why, we had been gently led to this very rocking chair!

Pause here with me for a few moments, friend, so that the Lord's goodness can overtake us. The Lord foreknows the details of our lives. If God is powerful enough to know the future, then isn't He completely able to walk us through it?

I was profoundly comforted by this sudden revelation, but I also knew God was not assuring me that Samuel would recover. As I rocked that morning, I went on to wonder whether the Shepherd meant to carry Samuel on into Heaven. All I knew for sure was that the Lord would carry my baby close to His heart and gently lead me—and that was enough.

Hospital day one and then two crept by. Samuel was well cared for but not bouncing back as I had hoped. On the afternoon of day three, I glanced at Samuel's sweet face in the hospital crib to see his eyes fixed and desperate, then watched helplessly as his face turned blue amidst blaring monitors. Our new roommate, the young mother of the newborn baby girl in the next crib, stepped around the amassing hospital staff, slipped her arm around my waist and whispered, "Do you want me to pray?" I couldn't form a word, much less a prayer, so I nodded assent. (Thank goodness for intercessors in times of crisis. The answers to their prayers uphold us.)

All eyes were on Samuel. The circle round the crib willed Him to breathe. In the weighty pause I heard the Lord instruct, "Turn up the oxygen." The injunction was so strong I said aloud, "Should we turn up the oxygen?" One nurse shook her head, "No, wait." Another long pause—I had just determined to dive over her and do it myself when another staff member reached over Samuel's head and cranked the oxygen output lever. Immediately Samuel drew a breath. After a lifetime of minutes, the second crisis was past.

On the fifth day, armed with a new nebulizer—I hoped I could assemble, and CPR instruction—I hoped I could remember, we were discharged. Samuel was by no means well. He still had double pneumonia and needed constant care. We placed his portable crib near our bed and propped the mattress at a thirty-degree angle.

Breathing treatments were administered every four hours along with prescription medication, but I could see no marked improvement in the days that followed. The nights were the worst for me. Emotionally and physically exhausted as I was, I could hardly close my eyes. In his fragile state, I was afraid that Samuel would die while I was asleep. When he had stopped breathing at the hospital, there had been monitors to alert the nursing staff. I was terrified that the same scenario would play out in my dark bedroom and no one would respond.

It was during these difficult weeks that I received a call from my friend Martha. She offered to host a game night at her house for our children, care for Samuel, and send Richard and me away with a picnic dinner. I was thankful for her kindness but also apprehensive about leaving Samuel. Richard encouraged me to accept the gift, and I finally agreed.

After depositing the children and collecting the dinner basket, Richard and I opened the feast on the lawn of a near-by park. It was gourmet in every way with appetizers, homemade soup in a thermos, and chocolate-dipped strawberries. Despite the beautiful setting and food, I felt that if I relaxed, my body would crack. The Lord's sweet promise to carry Samuel and lead me seemed like a lifetime ago. I had reached emotional bankruptcy, which is the perfect place for the power of God to enter.

As we were returning the remains of the meal to the basket, I remembered something else—something very, very valuable. The Lord would certainly speak to me if I asked. In my spirit I turned to face Him, knowing from experience that He would comfort me and show me what to do. I decided to fast and pray until He spoke. It was as easy as sighing, and in essence it was a spiritual sigh followed by a deep gulp of hope. I deliberately leaned back into the Lord.

On the morning of the second day of the fast, just as I was waking, He spoke three words, "light, momentary trouble." Reaching once more for my Bible, I found the passage that included those words. "Therefore we do not lose heart. Though outwardly we are wasting away, yet inwardly we are being renewed day by day. For our *light and momentary troubles* are achieving for us an eternal glory that far outweighs them all (2 Cor. 4:16–17, emphasis mine). I understood (even though this was not exactly the central theme of this passage) that what Samuel and I were facing now would seem light and momentary in retrospect, and that Samuel was being "renewed inwardly day by day." This season would surely pass, and Samuel would live. It's something that I knew as undeniable fact. It was a promise received by faith.

Prayers That Must Defined

At the time of Samuel's crisis, the Lord shepherded me with His voice. *He* initiated the conversation that continued over many dark, precarious weeks. As I recognized and applied His revelation, I had knowledge and peace beyond my natural understanding. Looking back I can clearly see that God has steadfastly guided me, not just during Samuel's illness, but all the days of my life.

Isn't it logical that the One who calls Himself the Word is always communicating (John 1:1)? And that He, who created us to commune with Him, sacrificed Himself so that we could return to Him, and knows what we will say before we say it, *likes* to hear our voice talking to Him (Song 2:14)? Thankfully, this most meaningful of all conversations is never based on our goodness, achievements, or the quality of our questions. The privilege of hearing and being heard is based on the sacrifice of Jesus alone. Timid voice, bold words, speechless longing—no matter—the glad welcome is still the same!

"Prayers that *must*" is my term for this vital, rich two-way communication with God. The conversation begins when the Lord reaches for us. God is Love and His love *must* reach for relationship. Our responsibility is to recognize His voice and respond to Him. Then He faithfully replies. In the interlude we enjoy His presence, obey, and trust. These are fresh prayers offered in garden-style simplicity. (See Adam and Eve talk with God in the Garden of Eden in Gen. 3:14–18.) I think this running conversation is what Paul encouraged when he said to "pray continually" (1 Thess. 5:17). We are either listening to the Lord or expressing something to Him and waiting in anticipation for His response. This is the duty and joy of our lives. Eventually, we find that we can't live without the Lord of the conversation. We simply *must* pray.

Prayers that must (conversational prayer) are indispensably edifying and strengthening. They introduce wisdom and bequeath peace. When we do not know how to proceed, they're the next reasonable step. They are a relief. They are easy. They are rest.

Herein lies the difference between *prayers that must* and the very valuable *discipline of prayer*. Spiritual disciplines are driven by initiative, strong spiritual hunger and perseverance. Eventually they break through to a spiritual habit. My garage meetings with the Holy Spirit, shared in chapter two, were a prayer discipline. But prayers that must are a natural response to our need to have communion and communication with God—right now. The only discipline required is remembering to pray and learning to listen well. Acquiring these tools is the focus of the rest of this book.

Like Tevya's candid conversations with God in *Fiddler on the Roof*, we talk and listen all along our ordinary day. The Lord is ever calling and waiting for our focus to shift. I have often wondered why it takes us so long to lean into the relationship. When we turn, there we are in the midst of Him—The Answer.

His Voice

When God pressed the Isaiah and 2 Corinthians passages into my consciousness in Samuel's crisis, I knew He was speaking because I recognized His voice. Perceiving and enjoying His voice has become the most exciting adventure of my life. His voice brings His essence and embrace. As He speaks, He overwhelms me with His love. So perceiving His voice is an encounter with Him.

Experience has proved that I needn't fear that Jesus will speak because His voice brings His presence, and His Person is always kind—even when correcting (Rom. 2:4). He honors like a bridegroom honors His bride. His consistent goodness teaches me to trust Him.

My first indication that the Lord is speaking is that His voice arrests my attention. Sometimes His communication is unmistakable. But His words can also sound like my own thoughts and imagination or the input of those around me. Then I wonder, "Is the Lord speaking or am I only beguiled by my own mind, will, and emotions?"

I asked the Lord once about the dilemma of identifying His voice. What He revealed surprised me. He said that ninety percent of the time when I stopped long enough to wonder if He was speaking, it was indeed His voice! Then I was horrified because I had so often dismissed these unctions resulting in blatant disobedience. My rule: If I have to stop and ask, "Is this the Lord?"—it is probably God! Discernment about how to proceed then follows the acknowledgement that He is speaking.

I now long for the Lord's communication. His thoughts are pure wisdom, so opposite my natural inclinations (Isa. 55:8–9). When He speaks, He brings truth to bear, broadening my limited understanding with His counsel. In the midst of His fresh revelation or instruction, I often find my understanding has shifted so unexpectedly that one moment I do not know, I am not aware; the next moment I know something so conclusively that I involuntarily say, "Oh! Now I understand."

As my spirit perceives His communication and immanent presence, peace often enters and spreads out, or pure joy bubbles up from within. Unbidden tears can follow. I think it is His kindness that invokes a response at many levels. When He speaks, I find that I *must* respond, which becomes the next segment of our ongoing conversation.

In the next two chapters I share some of the ways the Lord speaks, but I want to emphasize that His voice is consistently wrapped in the package of His written Word. Even when His words do not express exact terms from the Bible, what I perceive as His voice is reflected and confirmed by His written Word and holy character. The Scriptures are a record of what the Lord has done and said in the past, and He doesn't change (Heb. 13:8, Mal. 3:6–7). He is true to Himself.

The Rest of the Story

In the years after Jesus graciously spoke about Samuel's life and brought him to full health, I was still haunted by the reoccurring memory of Samuel's baby face, so desperate on hospital day three, as he struggled to draw a breath. The scene came to me most often in the middle of the night. As his face appeared, the same sick terror poured over me like acid, every bit as potent as the moment of the actual event. This sporadic memory became a form of emotional torture.

One early morning during a time of private prayer, the little face appeared again, but this time the vision panned out to reveal significant missing information. To my amazement I saw a hand gently, but authoritatively placed on Samuel's forehead. In the few spiritual visions I have experienced, I was supernaturally given the ability to understand things about the scene that were not articulated with words. I knew that the hand in the draping white sleeve was the hand of Jesus. I further knew that nothing—no virus or complication—could have taken Samuel's life unless the Lord had permitted it. He had been in control every moment. With that knowledge peace entered and changed the power of that memory to hurt me.

Since the life of prayer is our spiritual oxygen, I wonder if prayerlessness looks like Samuel's precious little face when he could not take a breath. Just as the Lord was standing near Samuel in his helplessness, we can be assured that He is near us when we cannot or will not pray. His strength, not ours, initiates and sustains the relationship. Our reasonable response is to relax back into spiritual breath, the oxygen of prayer, and let Him teach us to recognize and respond to His voice.

Going Deeper
Questions for Small Group Discussion

1. How do you differentiate between God's voice and your own thoughts? How do you know when He is speaking to you?
He is often abrupt and I know that ———→

2. When did God's voice change your perception of a challenge you had to face? When God refuted my negative reaction with the truth.

3. Describe a time when you couldn't pray. Who prayed for you when you couldn't form a prayer of your own?

4. Prayer that must or conversational prayer is defined as a running conversation with God spread over all the ordinary days of our

lives into eternity. Describe a conversational prayer—God's part and your part.

5. Have you ever been afraid to hear God's voice? Do you know why? If the Lord's voice doesn't feel safe consider reading the chapter "The Prayer That Must Have Truth" in Part Three of this book. When I fear He will ask me to do or say something that is too hard or will humiliate me.

I could not have come up with this thought, solution or word. It is often simple and perfect, exactly what I needed.

How the Lord Speaks

I love the Lord, for he heard my voice;
he heard my cry for mercy.
Because he turned his ear to me,
I will call on him as long as I live.
Ps. 116:1

It was just before sunrise on the morning of September 26, 2006, downtown Oklahoma City. Having slept little during the night, I was already awake and alert when I heard a screechy stretcher being wheeled toward my hospital room. Bumping around a tight corner, it halted at my bedside. As I slipped to the stretcher for transport to surgery, my faithful mom startled up from the recliner where she had spent an uncomfortable night and came to my side.

I was to have the privilege of giving one of my healthy kidneys to our now eleven-year-old son Samuel, who was in kidney failure and on dialysis. Richard, who had spent the night in Samuel's room at Oklahoma University Children's Hospital, the next building over, was simultaneously seeing Samuel off for surgery.

I had been through many months of every conceivable medical and mental procedure to be cleared for this opportunity, finally being declared healthy enough in body (hurray) and mentally sane (that was certainly good to know), but I was terrified, not jubilant. I had hoped I would be brave.

As we squeezed into the elevator and entered an austere pre-op room, my continuous, silent tears soaked the thin stretcher pillow. I couldn't will myself to stop crying and was embarrassed because there were several other people in the room awaiting surgery. They all seemed at peace. Swallowing hard barely saved me from sobbing out loud.

Seeing my obvious distress, several kind staff persons smiled at me or took my hand for a moment before hurrying away to attend to their various duties. Minutes before surgery, one of the assisting surgeons bent over the stretcher and patted my hand. While he chatted congenially, I fastened my complete attention on his face. He was obviously trying to help, and I was desperate. In a broken Caribbean accent he gave me this final encouragement: "You will be fine. This is easy surgery. You skinny. I've done hard surgeries." He continued to pat as he spoke. "You skinny; you do very well!" I remember thinking, "He thinks I'm skinny? I must look deceptively frail lying here on this stretcher." I tried to smile through my tears, but nothing stopped the sick terror that threatened to suffocate me. In truth I believed I was about to die.

This story is not really about me—or even Samuel. It's about God's faithfulness to both of us during the many months of uncertainty that preceded the kidney transplant. It is about His willingness to speak in personal ways and the strong comfort of His voice.

This adventure in prayer began almost two years before the day of our dual surgery. Through the fall of 2004 and into January 2005, Samuel began having blinding migraine headaches that continued to increase in severity and frequency. When no over the counter remedy could touch the pain, we sought medical advice, inadvertently discovering that his blood pressure was raging. The headache mystery was solved, but why would a child have dangerously high blood pressure? After being referred to a pediatric nephrologist by a pediatric cardiologist, Samuel was finally diagnosed with the beginning stages of renal failure associated with a rare syndrome.

As the months passed, his kidney function continued to decline until July of 2006 when I was trained to administer peritoneal dialysis at home. Dialysis made a definite difference in his health, but we were already discussing a kidney transplant. A kidney from a family member appeared to be his best option. As I seemed to be the only family member to fit all of the stringent qualifications for organ donation, I began the process of being medically cleared for the surgery and was eventually granted permission to donate.

But not long after, I began to have a sinking sense about giving my kidney. I think I was afraid that so drastic a procedure would either end my life or be the beginning of the end. I had no medical reason to believe such a lie, but it still sickened me in reflective moments.

The Lord is my confidant, the wisest person I know. I sought Him for assurance and strength, knowing He would speak to me. And in answer, He deliberately spoke on three separate occasions as I awaited the surgery date.

The first wave of comfort came late that summer. I had specifically asked the Lord to speak to my growing fear and was listening for His answer. Early one morning, unexpectedly, I was humming a hymn that I had not sung in a long, long time. It sounded like an echo that was increasing in volume. I knew—as we seem to know in these moments—that the Lord wanted me to pay attention. By intentionally humming through again and again, I was finally able to remember the first few words of the first line.

Hurrying to my old, red Methodist hymnal and turning to the index of first lines, I found the hymn, "Praise to the Lord, the Almighty." With rising curiosity I sang every verse aloud, letting His specially chosen words minister to me. Here is the song Jesus used to answer my specific prayer. I italicized the lines that brought the revelation of His comfort.

Praise to the Lord, the Almighty[5]

Praise to the Lord, the Almighty, the King of creation!
O my soul, praise him, for *He is thy health and salvation!*
All ye who hear now to his temple draw near; join me in glad adoration!

Praise to the Lord, who o'er all things so wondrously reigneth
Shelters thee under His wings, yea, so gently sustaineth,
Hast thou not seen how thy desires have been e'er granted in what He ordaineth?

Praise to the Lord, who doth prosper thy work and defend thee;
Surely his goodness and mercy here daily attend thee.
Ponder anew what the Almighty can do if with His love He befriend thee.

Praise to the Lord! Oh, let all that is in me adore Him!
All that has life and breath, come now with praises before Him!
Let the amen sound from his people again. Gladly forever adore Him!

The whole song anointed me like fragrant oil, but in particular, I understood that giving a kidney was "ordained for me" and that in so doing "all my longings" for Samuel's long-term health would be provided. All that was left to do was to "let the amen" (so be it) sound from my spirit and adore Him, which I did profusely!

Now you would think that His word for me would have been enough, and it was—for a few weeks. Then the second round of apprehension surfaced, and I was right back where I had begun. By this time we were just a week from the surgery date.

That fall Richard and I were once again helping facilitate the Bible study, *Experiencing God, Knowing and Doing the Will of God* through our church. During the small group breakout, we shared that the following week we would be absent due to the upcoming transplant.

Sitting directly across from me in that small circle was a doctor and his wife, who were visiting our church, and who I didn't know personally. Looking intently at me, he stated with conviction, "Giving a kidney is the gift of life! I know because my brother gave me his kidney. It's the most wonderful gift I've ever received. He literally saved my life." As he shared this testimony, he impacted me with the magnitude of his gratefulness. How his words braced and visioned me! His joy was contagious, and I caught it on the spot.

That couple was only active in our church for that short period of time, and as far as I know, never returned. I believe the Lord planted that man there for *me* that night. Wherever he is now, bless him, Jesus.

The Lord's final encouragement came the night before the surgery, just hours before the stretcher arrived. It was the middle of the night. My mother was asleep in the recliner just to my right. In preparation for an early morning transplant, I was hooked up to an IV drip, and its monitor was the only light in the room. Foreboding tortured my mind as I tossed restlessly, often staring into the darkness with wide-open eyes.

Silently I cried out to the Lord. "Speak! Comfort me. I need You. Oh, how I need You." Finally, I glanced at the bedside table where my study and worship materials were stored for the hospital stay. Selecting *Experiencing God* from the middle of the stack, I opened the well-worn workbook to the page where I had left off a few days before, hoping to stay current with the class. By leaning forward and positioning the workbook under the light of the monitor, I was just able to make out the text. My eyes fell immediately on the bottom half of the left page and I read, "Now choose life, so that you and your children may live and that you may love the LORD your God, listen to his voice, and hold fast to him. For the LORD is your life, and He will give you many years in the land He swore to give to your fathers, Abraham, Isaac and Jacob" (Deut. 30:19b–20).

Obviously the context of this passage has nothing to do with kidney transplants, but you can imagine how I interpreted the choices and promises laid so clearly before me . . . and as I have already shared, I still cried all the way to surgery!

People who donate an organ are lauded as heroes, but I don't deserve the title. The hero of this testimony is the Lord, who spoke to me in my deep need and brought Samuel and me to a place of healing.

Samuel is now 10 years plus with his new kidney and doing well. Don't tell my surgeon, but I was up to walking four miles a day (very, very slowly) exactly one week after my surgery and have continued in good health as well. Everything the Lord said to me was completely true. I have seen all that I longed for "granted in what He ordaineth." The kidney donation has truly been "the gift of life," just as I was told it would be. Most importantly, I have seen first hand that the Lord *is* my life.

How the Lord Speaks

As I shared in Part One, our Father speaks through His Son, His Spirit, and His written Word. These are the foundational conduits of all holy conversation. But the conversation is by no means locked into a single style. One of the most interesting aspects of the Lord's voice is the way He tailors His guidance for each individual. Consider the diverse ways He revealed Himself in scripture:

- Adam and Eve—walking and talking in the Garden of Eden, warnings and consequences, prophecy
- Abraham—straight talk with demonstrations of covenant, examples from nature, a test of obedience
- Jacob—a dream, restated covenant, long years of training, a wrestling match
- Joseph—dreams, trying circumstances, Pharaoh's dream accompanied by the wisdom to act on it
- Moses—the Angel of the Lord in a burning bush, miracles, face-to-face conversation, a mentor
- Gideon—the Angel of the Lord, a fleece test, a water test
- Balaam—a donkey, an angel
- Elijah—fire from Heaven, the still small voice, illustrations
- Esther—the encouragement of her uncle, the favor of a Gentile king
- David—The Law, worship, a prophet
- Nebuchadnezzar—a dream, a prophet, a testing period of insanity
- Belshazzar—writing on a wall with a divine hand
- Darius—his friend's example, a miracle of protection
- Jonah—the Lord's command to go and preach, a storm, divine rescue, a vine illustration
- Mary and Joseph—an angel, dreams, the testimony of others, prophecy, Jesus
- Peter—parables, miracles, a coin in a fish's mouth, a huge catch of fish, a cock's crow, the Holy Spirit
- Paul—the Law, the audible voice of Jesus in the midst of a blinding light, a messenger, the apostles in Jerusalem, visions, the Holy Spirit

How surprised Jacob must have been to find himself at the base of a staircase that ascended to Heaven. No one else in the Bible saw the staircase (Gen. 28:10–19). Moses saw the angel of the Lord in a burning bush. What an unusual way to arrest his attention (Ex. 3:1–6). Balaam received a shock when his donkey spoke, revealing that an angel had drawn a sword to kill him. No one else was given such a bizarre, supernatural warning (Num. 22:21–31).

In the months before Samuel's kidney transplant, the Holy Spirit used a hymn, a testimony, and His Word quoted in a workbook to intentionally speak to me. I am often singing but not hazy hymns from my childhood. I hear many testimonies, but not from kidney transplant recipients. I often do Bible studies and read Scripture, but not the instruction to "choose life that my children may live" just hours before an organ donation to my son. My Father used ordinary means in extraordinarily personal ways.

The Lord communicates profusely. Because He knows the details of our preferences and personality, He customizes the means to impact us, just as He did in the lives of Bible heroes long ago. The Lord never hides His will or withholds His wisdom. I am humbled by the Lord's mercy. He willingly counsels us as we sit at home and walk along the road and lie down and get up (Deut. 6:7). And in so doing, He guides us with His love.

Going Deeper
Questions for Small Group Discussion

1. When has the Lord used music to speak to you? Share about the impact of His communication. *Random worship songs from long ago, long forgotten.*

2. When has the Holy Spirit highlighted a specific Bible verse or passage to guide or comfort you?

3. Who has spoken into your life just when you needed it? How did you apply the wisdom shared?

4. Think back over your favorite Bible studies or other study pursuits. Which ones have had a lasting benefit? What did you learn?

5. God honors our unique personalities because He created them! How has God tailored His communication to best impact your life?

In the Midst of His Voice

Prophecy

In that day the Branch of the Lord will be beautiful and glorious, and the fruit of the land will be the pride and glory of the survivors in Israel.

Isa. 4:2

A Mentor's Advice

When Esther's words were reported to Mordecai, he sent back this answer: "Do not think that because you are in the king's house you alone of all the Jews will escape. For if you remain silent at this time, relief and deliverance for the Jews will arise from another place, but you and your father's family will perish. And who knows but that you have come to your royal position for such a time as this?"

Est. 4:12–14

A Dream

[Joseph] said to them, "Listen to this dream I had: We were binding sheaves of grain out in the field when suddenly my sheaf rose and stood upright, while your sheaves gathered around mine and bowed down to it."

Gen. 37:6–7

A Vision

During the night Paul had a vision of a man of Macedonia standing and begging him, "Come over to Macedonia and help us."

Acts 16:9

A number of years ago my husband and I received an opportunity through his company to take an Alaskan cruise. The trip happened to fall the month before our twentieth wedding anniversary. Despite our exceeding joy at this unexpected gift, it was a trip that I almost didn't take. During this season of my life, I was drowning in home school and struggling with persistent depression. Burnout had singed my zeal for life. Besides, people with seven children don't leave town without them. Who would volunteer to keep them? But encouraged by my husband and aided by the kind help of my mother-in-law and sister-in-law, the arrangements were eventually completed.

When we had finally boarded the ship docked in Vancouver and were ascending to our cabin level in the ship's central glass elevator, I suddenly became aware of the dear strains of a familiar melody. Rising through the open nine-story atrium from a live string quartet at ground level was my favorite piece of music ever written, "Jesu, Joy of Man's Desiring," by J. S. Bach.[7] This particular piece played on my favorite instruments in that exact moment was so personal, so thoughtful. It was the Lord! As I acknowledged His voice, He affirmed that He had planned this trip for me, and I was to receive it directly from His hand. Blinded by sudden tears, I worshipped Him.

There were thousands of passengers welcomed aboard by that concert as it echoed up staircases and down corridors. There were probably those who greatly appreciated the excellence of the quartet, even those who loved that particular piece of music for reasons of their own. But most never noticed the song and certainly don't treasure the memory today. Why should they? That song was a gift for me.

Meditate with me for a moment on the intentionality of the Lord in this deceptively simple spiritual encounter. Let's consider first a particular quartet hired for the afternoon boarding process of a particular cruise ship at a given hour. Consider the quartet's freedom to select popular classical music and arrange the pieces as they pleased for the concert. Now consider the details of my situation in life: my emotional state, my personality, even my musical preferences. Finally, see me in line dockside, being

processed through customs and stepping onto the boarding deck—
right on cue.

This is a peek at the backstage preparation of a single encounter on behalf of a single individual by an extraordinary God. What intentionality on the Lord's part! Can we doubt that He is willing to go to great lengths to delight, guide, astound, and change us?

The Bible is filled with similar accounts of God's creative, strategic interaction with people. In this chapter I would like to highlight a few of the Word's most-mentioned methods of revelation: prophecy, mentors, dreams, and visions. God sovereignly uses these when He wants us to have specific information. They come at His discretion—not ours—to bring clarity. To God be the glory!

Prophecy

A prophecy is a divine revelation inspired by God. A word of prophecy may or may not relate to the future. The Holy Spirit has definitely given precedence to prophecy—whole books of the Bible showcase His glad tidings and dire warnings.

Some revelation was understood and heeded: People course-corrected and were blessed. Of course, the opposite was also true: People ignored some prophecy and suffered the consequences.

Still other prophecies were announced, but the meaning left shrouded, sealed for another generation; these prophecies helped people stay alert throughout generations of watching, watching, watching for their fulfillment.

In the Gospels, Jesus predicted His own death and resurrection, the coming of the Holy Spirit, the fall of Jerusalem, and the signs of the end of the age. The early Church was often guided by prophecy, and Paul listed it with other spiritual gifts in 1 Corinthians 12:10. All valid prophecy brings glory to the Lord by proving His sovereignty, justice, and mercy.

The Lord sometimes equips and encourages me through prophecy. These prophetic words are nuggets of encouragement and godly perspective either directly from the Lord in His gentle whisper (1 Kings 19:12), or from a trusted friend. Often they come when I am quiet and seeking in prayer and can be applied to something I am experiencing.

Once in a while a prophecy is wisdom for something that is about to happen. When I am shocked or overwhelmed, the first question I ask myself is, "What was the last thing the Lord emphatically said to me?" Looking back a page or two in my journal, I can often see His instruction. My faith is greatly strengthened when I perceive that my Father is in control of the details of my life. The following examples show how God brought revelation ahead of events that braced me in the midst of them.

One afternoon I was reading *Prince Caspian*, one of the seven books in *The Chronicles of Narnia*, by C. S. Lewis[8]—it must have been for the fifth time. Reading along in pure pleasure, I came to the place in the novel where Lucy and her siblings: Peter, Edmund, Susan, and their friend Trumpkin are lost in the woods, hopelessly traveling in circles.

Suddenly Lucy sees Aslan, who represents Jesus in the story. He beckons her to follow Him over the edge of a treacherous ravine. Lucy alone sees Aslan. When she explains who she has seen and His instructions, the majority decide to ignore Lucy's plea and continue with their own plan—what little plan there is. None of the rest of them sees Aslan after all, and plummeting over the edge of a ravine is just not attractive enough to lure them. Lucy cries bitterly as she follows them away from the place Aslan has instructed them to go.

Now, as I reread this portion of the story that day, I began to weep too. At first it was just a tear and a sniff, but these were soon followed by torrents of blinding tears and wrenching sobs. I distinctly remember thinking, "What is wrong with me?" I knew that so familiar a plot couldn't have invoked such a strong emotional reaction.

I have since learned that when I'm suddenly grieved to tears with no apparent reason, the Holy Spirit is grieved and expressing His emotion through me. I sensed that the Lord was speaking, but I didn't know what He was saying. Later He revealed it.

In the next months I had a personal experience that paralleled the scene in *Prince Caspian*. I was teaching in a Sunday School setting. The study I had written encouraged movement towards intimacy with the Lord and deeper worship. This type of teaching was new to some of my friends—alarmingly new, almost like suggesting that we all walk over the side of a cliff. Looking back, I can see their point. Who was I to issue a directive and why should they believe me? To my sorrow, I now realize that I also lacked humility in my presentation.

Unbeknownst to me, some of the class discussed the situation and decided to ask me to step out of leadership. I received an unexpected phone call from a spokesperson and immediately stepped down as requested. Later some of the members broke from the class. I felt responsible and was sickened.

When the worst of the pain of rejection had passed, the Lord reminded me of my unexpected tears over Lucy's plight months before and revealed that He had foreknown that this rift would hurt us all. Imagine a God who grieves in advance for our personal pain. He cares that much. Pause, and think reverently of that.

Later in the Prince Caspian narrative, Aslan appears again and safely leads the children down that very same ravine by way of a concealed path. The same was true of those in the Sunday School rift. In the end the Lord faithfully guided each of us into the next season of our spiritual lives. We were all blessed. He does all things well.

On another occasion I was spiritually primed for an event that would take me to my knees. As I was preparing for bed one night, the Lord quite simply said, "Hold on." There was nothing ominous in the intonation of the phrase. I keep a journal on the bedside table. Flipping to a clear spot, I scribbled, "Hold on." As I did, I sensed that the phrase was His invitation for a deeper study with interesting prospects. I happened to wake early the next morning and my first thought was to slip to the family room and study that phrase. I thoroughly enjoyed the study discovering that the Lord directs us to hold on to specific things: to what is good, godly instruction, words of life, faith, etc.

The next afternoon Richard and I received news of a desperate family crisis. After hours of deep turmoil, late, late into the night, I found myself weeping on my knees in the middle of the family room floor. Desperately, I thought back, "What was the last thing the Lord said to me?" Can you imagine what "hold on" meant to me in that moment? It was the courage to stand up and begin again.

The Lord's Wisdom through Mentors

Many times the Lord speaks through family, friends, pastors, or even authors we will never meet. Just as the Word of the Lord came to David through Jonathan, to Esther through her uncle Mordecai, and to Timothy through Paul, we can be deeply impacted by the encouragement and example of others.

I could share pages of truths gained sitting at the feet of mentors; indeed my journals are packed with this type of wisdom, but I will confine myself to one.

A few years ago I had the privilege of meeting several times with a mentor whose insights have proven so practical. When I asked her about my tendency to step into leadership, and then wish I could pull back, she explained that what begins in confident faith can fizzle into self-doubt. The spirit leaps and soars while the cringing soul sputters, "What were you thinking? Why did you take such a risk? For heaven's sake, go back!"

To illustrate, she pulled a chair into the center of the room and stepped up onto the seat to represent accepting a new leadership opportunity. She encouraged that when the Lord invites me to "step up," I should gird enough courage to stand in faith and take in the view from the new position. Then, if the Lord so leads, command my soul to step up beside my faith-filled spirit instead of allowing my soul to demand a hasty retreat.

I still act on this advice. On occasions I have literally gone alone to the physical room that represented a leadership challenge, placed a chair in the middle of the floor and stepped up onto its seat. From that vantage I took in the room and meditated on the place of authority to which the Lord had called me. Still perched atop, I prayed for others and myself. Then aloud, I commanded my soul to stand in the new position and be at peace. I said *yes* to the Lord and *no* to my doubts. That advice has become concrete wisdom for my life, the Lord's voice through a trusted mentor.

Dreams

The Scripture says that "old men will dream dreams and young men will see visions" (Joel 2:28, Acts 2:14–17) and records many instances of the Lord's perspective and instruction through dreams.

Consider Abimelech, Jacob, Laban, Pharaoh, Joseph, Nebuchadnezzar, Isaiah, Jeremiah, Joseph (Jesus' earthly father), Paul, and John.

I began to give credence to my dreams after reading *Dream Language*, by James Goll.[9] He suggests that sleeping and awakening, those hours when soul and body are quiet and separated from the voices *without*, are an open space for the Lord's voice *within*. He recommends keeping a bedside journal to record significant dreams.

Steps for recording a dream:
- Assign the dream a title for referencing.
- Date the dream and record any current circumstances that seem related to the dream.
- While the dream is still vivid, record the details of the setting, plot, characters, and action, as well as noting impressions and feelings, colors and numbers.
- Ask the Holy Spirit for the interpretation and record His impressions; seek the scriptures for clues to the dream's meaning.

Reverence for biblical precedent and respect for James Goll have given me the courage to ask God to speak to me though dreams. It doesn't happen often, but the Lord has definitely spoken to me in this impactful way.

One early morning I had a dream that I still treasure. In the dream I saw a dreary parking garage. As I watched, a friend trudged toward a parked car, opened the back door, and lifted her very fussy toddler into her car seat. The little girl was on the verge of a terrible tantrum, angry and kicking. Patiently, gently, firmly, my friend buckled the straps amidst much resistance. Finished at last, she fell into the driver's seat exhausted and defeated.

As I watched the scene, I was especially struck by her kind persistence, which I admired, and equally, her distraught frustration, which caused my empathy. I was feeling her emotion because I had once been the mother of toddlers. I could tell she believed that this season of her life would never end, but as an older mom who had successfully graduated "terrible" two-year-olds into other ages, I knew the truth—this was only a brief season of parenting. The rewards of her investment would bear fruit in the life of her daughter, but she must not give up (Gal. 6:9)!

I cared deeply that she was unable to know what I could plainly see, so in the dream I began calling to my friend, "Don't give up! You're doing great! Hold steady!" By her demeanor I could tell that she was unaware of my presence and deaf to my voice. Her discouragement insulated her from any thoughts and emotions, save her own. So I leaned forward and shouted encouragement with all my might. "You're going to make it! It's only a season, and it will end!"

As I watched, the friend began fumbling with her cell phone as though she had heard something indistinctly but wasn't sure of the source. She never did know who was speaking or what had been communicated. She drove away without wisdom's perspective.

On awakening I wrote the dream's narrative and its impressions. And throughout the morning I continued to prayerfully reflect on a possible meaning. Was a friend in need of encouragement—perhaps the very lady who had appeared in the dream? Did I need to be more intentional about speaking into the lives of young mothers in general?

A few hours later, the Lord shared the interpretation—I was shocked. My friend represented *me* in the dream, and *His* was the shouted voice of encouragement. The dream came to me not long after the horrendous family episode mentioned above, when I was sobbing in the family room floor in the middle of the night. In the aftermath the Lord had given me the strength to begin again, but even so I couldn't fathom a time when my relationships would be restored and my parenting fruitful. During these disorienting days, I had unknowingly blocked the Lord's repeated assurances with my negative self-talk, so He spoke to me through a dream. He wanted me to know that He cared deeply and that I would certainly pass to other seasons of life.

This interpretation had not occurred to me until the very moment the Holy Spirit revealed it. The insight gained is a lesson I have never forgotten because in a way, I lived it through the dream.

Visions

Another way the Lord encouraged, instructed, and corrected His people in the Old and New Testaments was through visions. "I spoke to the prophets, gave them many visions and told parables through them" (Hos. 12:10). The book of Acts records many visions that impacted the early Church; Stephen, Ananias, Cornelius, Peter, and Paul all saw visions.

Visions seem to come in a variety of intensities. Some are a very brief glimpse of a scene, like a spiritually significant bleep in the imagination. Others are longer with vivid scenes, action, and conversation. And still others are so real they are like a front row seat at a play with plenty of time to study the details of the backdrop, the clothes people are wearing, and the exact words being spoken.

God has used visions to bring revelation in my life, although these are rare. Mine have been in the "bleep" form. One in particular brought insight and guidance. In sharing it, I do not mean to dictate in any way what the Lord desires for your family. He guides our unique families according to His will and wisdom.

One Christmas when my younger children were small and the older ones were fast approaching their tweens, I became increasingly concerned about the way we celebrated Christmas. It all started when my homeschool friends began to bad mouth Santa Claus during one of our co-op's mommy-share times. Several voiced disgust with that tradition and the way it removed honor from the Lord.

Our family still celebrated Santa's visit on Christmas Eve, and I was secretly angry with my friends for being so "narrow." To make matters worse, their enlightened children kept indiscriminately announcing that there was no Santa, causing unwelcome questions at home.

The holiday season pleasantly passed despite this frustration, and the last week of December, I packed my misgivings away with the trimmings and forgot about them.

The following year as the Christmas boxes were dragged from the attic and reopened, so was that unresolved question about our family's tradition. My leftover defensiveness, pitted against my suspicion that my friends might have had a point, caused a clanking disturbance of spirit. Above all, I loved the Lord and wanted to please Him on His birthday. I was now ready to lay aside every other opinion save the Lord's and seek His will for our children.

Richard and I discussed the issue; then I asked for outside advice (avoiding those home school friends). I distinctly remember the afternoon in early December when I decided to call my mother for her perspective. As I washed the lunch dishes, phone between my shoulder and cheek, I outlined my dilemma. The conversation concluded with her final counsel, "Why does it have to be all or nothing? Why not let the *little* children have their Santa for now, even though the older children have outgrown him?"

I hung up the phone and dried my hands. Heading into another part of the house, still pondering her advice, the words "little children" continued to echo in my mind.

Suddenly the Lord brought a brief vision. I saw a scene in the imagination realm of my mind, but this was different because I didn't imagine it as an act of my will or remember it from a past experience.

In the vision Jesus was seated with a little girl on His lap. The child was perhaps four with shoulder-length brown hair. They were in conversation. She was gazing into His face as she spoke and He was listening with interest. As the intimate scene appeared, the Holy Spirit said, "Let the *little* children come to *Me*" (Mark 10:14, emphasis mine). As all these impressions registered, I was stricken by the sudden knowledge that the Lord was jealous for the child. (In *The Truth Project*,[10] Del Tackett defines the Lord's jealousy as anything that threatens covenant love.) I knew that Jesus longed for this little girl to come to Him with every need and desire. The vision appeared and was gone in the next moment.

It took two seconds to make a strong decision about Santa and our Christmas celebration—too strong, as you will see. Perceiving what I believed was the Lord's heart for our family on this matter, I determined not to seat my children with anyone save Jesus to ask for their heart's desire. Then in an extremely black and white decision, I also determined that I would eradicate Santa's image and every "secular" Christmas tradition from our home. Richard and I told the children the truth about Santa that very day, but the decoration transformation took several years to complete.

I began to incorporate Scripture and Christian symbols into our holiday decor little by little until finally, several Christmases later, I looked around the decorated house with relief. Everything pointed toward Jesus as Creator and Messiah or celebrated our family. I felt that the Lord was rightfully honored. Heading up the stairs with the last empty Christmas box to set away in the attic, I mentally congratulated myself for the transformation and thought, "Good riddance!" It was as if I were spiritually wiping dust from my hands.

Mid-step the Lord spoke. "Do not so lightly dismiss My saints!" I stopped to consider. I had treated St. Nicolas, as sinner-most-wanted, and the Lord was not pleased. St. Nicholas, a very righteous man, is in heaven now. He is not responsible for the degradation of our culture. I had gone too far, and the Lord had brought me back into balance. God used a vision and His voice to answer my specific question and correct me, and I am thankful.

Certainly prophecy, the advice of mentors, dreams, and visions must pass the test of spiritual discernment and the plumb line of Scripture before being applied to our lives, but I often find that they line up and bring the guidance that I need. Then I joyfully credit the Lord for counseling me. He chooses the means that best prepares, confirms, encourages, warns, comforts, corrects, and instructs us. Certainly, He hems us in behind and before, and places His hand upon us (Ps. 139:5). We are ever in the midst of His voice.

Going Deeper
Questions for Small Group Discussion

1. Which biblical prophecies build your faith in God's sovereignty? When has the Lord prepared or encouraged you through prophecy? Do you have the gift of prophecy? If so, how do you use that gift to bless others?

2. Who are your mentors? Have biblical heroes, authors, historical figures, or present day people led you by their words or example? What have those mentors spoken into your life? Do you mentor others? How has your experience or advice influenced their lives?

3. Do you value dreams? Why or why not? When has the Lord used a dream to guide or encourage you? Share the dream and its interpretation.

4. Has God used a vision to guide you? Describe the vision and how it impacted you.

Acting on the Lord's Voice

"Why do you call me, 'Lord, Lord,'
and do not do what I say?"
Luke 6:46

Back in the early nineties, Richard and I began to discuss the possibility of changing our church membership of almost ten years. Our church friends had become as dear as blood family, but we were longing for the worship style of our college days and felt that our family needed a church that was more open to the gifts of the Holy Spirit.

With three children under six, Richard did the preliminary church shopping for the family to lessen the trauma of unknown children's programs and foreign nurseries. He did some phone interviews with local pastors, while I asked lots of questions about the churches of our friends.

After many months, we had narrowed our prospective churches to two or three options and were prepared to launch our Sunday morning visits in person over the next weeks. I was relieved to have the decision close to being made. I may have understated that—I was rapturous at the thought of being released from our traditional church and had begun my countdown for the move.

In the meantime an event called *The Walk to Emmaus* was just being introduced in our church, and Richard and I had been accepted to attend. Emmaus is an interdenominational lay renewal movement with active communities in many areas of the United States and across the globe (emmaus.upperroom.org). Generally a renewal weekend is offered twice a year: Men attend the seventy-two hour retreat first (Thursday–Sunday evening), and the women's retreat follows two weekends later. We were excited about the opportunity to be away with the Lord in this "between churches" season.

Richard's seventy-two hours were a spiritually replenishing time for him—I could see it on his face when he came in the door that Sunday night. As he debriefed, I began to long for upcoming retreat in earnest.

Finally, he broached the subject matter he had tactfully saved for last. Speaking slowly and deliberately, he explained that during the retreat the Lord had revealed that we were not to leave our church; we were to stay planted. I stared in shocked silence. When I had words with which to reply, I vehemently sputtered that the Lord had certainly not revealed that fact to *me,* and that he had obviously missed God, to which he wisely responded that we would just wait and see. Convinced that he had been grievously deceived, I relegated the matter to the back of my mind, comforting myself with the thought that God would set him straight. (I'm being pretty transparent here. I hope other wives have never been this arrogant.)

My Emmaus experience was all Rich had described. The three days offered a time for everything under Heaven: A time to eat a lot and a time to sleep but little, a time to be creative and a time to enjoy the creativity of others, a time to laugh unrestrained and a time to weep healing tears, a time to lay down burdens and a time to take up disciplines. Woven all through the weekend was a broad immersion in the unconditional love of God.

About halfway through Sunday afternoon, as the retreat was in its final hours, the Lord spoke to me. I will never forget the experience. I was seated at a round table with six other ladies listening to their discussion about the testimony we had just heard. One moment I was blissfully unaware, and the next moment I understood conclusively: We were to stay at our home church. Period. The firm instruction was not stated in language, but it might as well have been. My predetermined will struck God's solid, immoveable will like a speeding car smashes into an iron barricade.

Shaken and sick, I began to cry tears of genuine grief. I cried and cried and cried. Just when I thought I had regained my composure, the tears spilled over again. Thankfully there was a box of Kleenex in the center of the table. About every minute and a half, I reached for a fresh tissue and added the soaked one to the growing pile before me. My obedience was requested. We were being asked to remain, but in that moment, I couldn't fathom God's reasoning. It took the perspective of many years to understand the *why*. In the meantime we chose to obey and stay.

Experiencing God through Obedience

Experiencing God, Knowing and Doing the Will of God, by Henry Blackaby and Claude V. King[11] contains an excellent description of the obedience process. According to Blackaby, each of us is called to walk in faith cycles that have similar steps:

1. God is at His work, advancing His Kingdom and pursuing each of us.
2. We are called to be in relationship with Him.
3. God invites us to join Him in His work.
4. The invitation to join God in a work that only He can perform, and the reality of our inability causes a crisis of belief.
5. By faith we must adjust our lives to join Him in His plan. The adjustment will require sacrifice.
6. As we obey, God accomplishes His work through us, and we come to know Him personally.
7. The more we know Him, the more He reveals what is on His heart, and the more willing we are to sacrifice for the honor of serving Him.

Blackaby uses the life of Moses to illustrate. God was at work in the days of Moses. Moved by the bitter oppression of the Israelites, He determined to deliver His people from Egyptian slavery. Moses was commissioned to join God in His plan at the burning bush. As God spoke, Moses knew for certain that God was speaking and exactly what He required. Even so, on the front side of the experience, Moses couldn't fathom how the situation could be changed. He had never seen God's power and provision to that extent. It was hard for Moses to ignore his personal weaknesses, but He placed His faith in the God of his ancestors Abraham, Isaac, and Jacob, and decided to obey. Sacrificial adjustments followed. As the deliverance unfolded, Moses saw Jehovah's power and provision firsthand, and the experience changed his understanding of the One who calls Himself *I Am*.

When God calls us—and He will—it is His invitation to join Him in Kingdom work that is impossible apart from His wisdom and power. That is why it requires faith. When we adjust our will to His, God does God-sized things through us and brings rightful glory to His name. As a result we know Him more. In addition, this priceless but arduous process strengthens our character and blesses others.

Promptings

The Lord's voice is not always as loud as it was at the burning bush. Sometimes the Holy Spirit only whispers (1 Kings 19:12). In instances where He quietly indicates concern, it is a very good idea to promptly separate ourselves from the potential snare. Equally, when He quietly indicates blessing, we can choose to obey and step into that opportunity by faith. The Lord doesn't always repeat these unctions, so we must be attentive to His voice and act.

One mid-summer afternoon, I received a prompting that decisively altered my direction. Several of my children had been attending a small Christian school in our area. A board member, who was also a personal friend, called to ask if I would consider interviewing for a junior high writing instructor's position for the next school term.

What an unexpected notion. I remember well the mental weighing and balancing that took place behind my masked phone voice. First came the negatives: I had an *art* degree. I knew pitifully little about writing curriculums. I hadn't worked outside my home in years. Teaching classes outside our home would surely upset our stable family routine. This position would mean considerable work—boo! I wouldn't even know where to begin. And why would

I think that I would be hired over more competent teachers interviewing for the position?

Next came the possibilities: What if this was an opportunity to help compensate tuition? Even a little would bless the family budget. Even more, I loved to teach and was good at it. An opportunity to teach outside my home could be a welcome challenge—hurray! If God had chosen me for this position, wouldn't His wisdom and power accompany the assignment?

In that tangled moment, the Lord spoke. It was as if His hand pressed my shoulder—only once and softly. That was all. He indicated that to interview for this particular job was the path of blessing.

I was hired within the month. Within two months the Lord had revealed the vision for the coursework. By the third, I was writing curriculum, interacting with students, and surprise— thoroughly enjoying the process. I now know that without this challenge, I wouldn't have had the skills or confidence to write this book. Many have been the blessings of this single step of obedience.

I have also ignored the Spirit's nudge. One prompting concerned a casual acquaintance made at a Christian women's outreach. A young woman named Sonia (not her real name) began to attend our monthly ministry meetings. One Friday afternoon she called unexpectedly. Her marriage was failing. I hardly knew this lady, but she wanted me to keep her preschool-aged daughter for the weekend, so she could "work on her marriage." I heard a quiet, but firm "no" from the Lord, but I brushed past it. I interpreted His warning as my own inhibition to get involved. Why would I shirk from serving a sister in need if it were in my power to bless her? The Lord had an opinion. I discerned His choice, but did it my way, forgetting that "to obey is better than sacrifice." (1 Sam. 15:22).

She called many times over the next year to "share" about her life, hint at her needs, and prod at my sentiments. Her voice over the phone caused a cringe, but I was ashamed of my judgments and repented. Her requests seemed odd, but I couldn't discern why. I sensed manipulation, but I set the impression away, doubly resolving to do the "Christian thing."

Later I discovered the truth. Sonia was a cunning pathological liar. Her pattern was to use up her Christian resources in one state before moving and starting over in a new place, always leaving destruction behind her. As soon as the information came to light, I saw the whole truth in a moment, yet hadn't I known not to trust her from the beginning? Then I realized to my horror that some of the pain experienced by her loved ones had been caused by my hapless assistance.

Daily life is like this—small choices coming at intervals. The Lord knows which decisions count. I have found that His indication can be a mere nod or shake of the head, a slight motion right or left. If I harden in the moment and resist Him, I can miss my cue, causing frustration and pain. Jesus' words are true: "Therefore everyone who hears these words of mine and puts them into practice is like a wise man who built his house on the rock" (Matt. 7:24).

The Blessing of Obedience

It has now been over twenty years since the Lord instructed Richard and me to stay planted in our church. It turned out that the Lord was not as interested in changing my church as He was in changing me! This next season began with a personal revival. (This was the time away with the Holy Spirit in my garage sanctuary mentioned in the chapter two.) What followed were deep cuts in my arrogant attitudes—ouch, followed by coursework in humility—double ouch. Some of my most cherished life lessons were gained because I obeyed, stayed, and was forced to learn them.

To my surprise our church also underwent reconstruction in God's gentle timing. It is interesting to note that *The Walk to Emmaus* retreat and *Experiencing God* Bible study mentioned above played a major role in the transformation of our whole church in those years.

If we had left when I wanted so desperately to go, I would never have known from experience how beautiful it is to pray over the long term and see a miraculous work that only God can do. I wouldn't have known the Lord in the deep and delightful ways He revealed Himself in those difficult years. Now I conclusively know from personal experience that the Lord can change anyone—even me. And seeing revival with my own eyes was well worth the wait. Blessing always follows obedience.

> . . . *eye has not seen and ear has not heard and has not entered into the heart of man, [all that] God has prepared (made and keeps ready) for those who love Him [who hold Him in affectionate reverence, promptly obeying Him and gratefully recognizing the benefits He has bestowed].* I Cor. 2:9 AMPC

In Part Two, we have discussed the beauty of the Lord's voice and the importance of conversational prayer—we *must* pray. In Part Three, let's delve into practical avenues of prayer that unveil our Father's love for each of us.

Going Deeper
Questions for Small Group Discussion

1. When has God's will collided with your will? Were you able to submit to His instruction? Is He currently asking you to submit to Him?

2. When has God asked you to join Him in His work? What was on His heart? How did He use your life to perform His will?

3. There is a faith-filled place between joining God in a work that only He can perform and the frustrating reality of our inability. When have you experienced this "crisis of belief"?

4. Have you ever had to adjust your life to follow God's plan? What steps did you take to align yourself with His new direction? Did it require personal sacrifices?

5. When have you experienced an indication of God's concern or blessing? How did you respond to His whisper?

PART THREE

Channels of Conversational Prayer

. . . pray continually, give thanks in all circumstances;
for this is God's will for you in Christ Jesus.
1 Thess. 5:17-18

The Prayer That Must Know
Walking in Love

Whether you turn to the right or to the left,
your ears will hear a voice behind you, saying,
"This is the way; walk in it."
Isa. 30:21

The crossroads of life can be so confusing. We can't know what a decision we make now may mean in the future. But in some cases we *must* know now, to proceed wisely. Such was my dilemma one summer as I prepared for a new school year.

As a homeschool mom, I use part of my summers to set goals and order curriculum. The summer of 1999 was no different, except I was doubly focused because I was expecting our seventh baby in October. I had to think through everything carefully before I didn't have time to think anymore.

After choosing a math curriculum, setting character goals, and designing a daily schedule, one weighty decision remained. Samuel, who was just turning four, was struggling with speech. I suspected that speech therapy would help. But in a school schedule where something as benign as taking a phone call could wreck all, middle-of-the-day appointments could potentially stretch the family to distraction. I was barely holding school together as it was; how could I take on anything more? On the other hand, what if this year was Samuel's best language acquisition window, and I foolishly let him suffer because I was too lazy to take him to a simple class? His speech was infinitely more important than my convenience.

The Lord often requires that we come to places like this, where we're stripped of our confidence in personal skill and reasoning, as well as these attributes in others. Worldly wisdom can never take us to the level of supernatural knowledge—things that only God knows, which brings us to the prayer that must know. In Samuel's speech therapy query, I simply didn't know what was the wisest course, but I had to know, and I knew that the Lord knew and was willing to tell me.

Narrowing the Question

In essence the prayer that must know is an act of humility. It often comes at the dead end of ourselves. Looking up, we remember that our Father cares about our details and would certainly speak if we asked Him. How could we have forgotten? At this place I have found it helpful to articulate a specific question and write it down. What exactly must be known? This is not so God can understand the question, but so that we will recognize the answer. By asking Him questions, we seek His face and cultivate attentiveness to His voice. We learn God's relational principles and prepare ourselves to obey Him without resisting.

I have heard it said that the mysteries of God are not hidden *from* us, but *for* us. In the prayer that must know, we seek hidden treasure purposefully stored for us to find. That the Lord will reveal His wisdom is a given "yes." This immanent surprise is, oh, such a joyous quest.

As I continued to debate the speech therapy question before me, I distinctly remember the Saturday afternoon that I headed out for a walk-and-talk with the Lord. I put it to Him this way: "Here's what I must know: Should Samuel have speech therapy this year, or should I wait until he's five?" It was that simple and that specific. Silence followed the articulation of the question, but I wasn't dismayed. The Lord would surely show me, and His answer would come in plenty of time for me to act on His instruction. I knew because He always had before. All that was left to do was wait in attentive anticipation. So I leaned forward expectantly.

Discerning His Voice

The next day was Sunday, and our family was in church as usual. When it was time for the sermon, instead of stepping into the pulpit from the platform, our pastor Jessica Moffatt surprised us by sweeping down the center aisle dressed in full costume as Suzanna Wesley (mother of John Wesley, founder of the Methodist denomination). In the monologue that followed, she described in first person English accent what it was like to be the mother of nineteen children. She described her dependence on God in times of death, narrow escapes, and miracles, as well as routine, persistent parenting. She mentioned different children by name and then came to her concern for her son *Samuel.* You can imagine that when she said that particular name, I sat up straighter. "Susanna" continued by explaining that Samuel Wesley was *five* years old and had never spoken a single word. Suddenly one day he began to talk in complete sentences!

Listening from my place in the third left pew, I was distinguishing the Lord's voice. "Samuel will not need to *speak* until he is five. Wait until next year for speech therapy." As our pastor continued her beautiful monologue, I was away with the Lord, wondering at the timing and details of this intricately fashioned answer to my very specific prayer. What peace, what confidence accompanied my plans for the fall. Samuel did take speech the following year, and his articulation dramatically improved.

After we have posed a question of the Lord, the moment comes when we believe the Lord is speaking. How do we know we are experiencing His voice and not our own?

Bible heroes inquired of the Lord and seemed to know that they were hearing His voice and exactly what He was saying. Knowing then birthed faith to act confidently on His instruction. Sometimes Jehovah spoke directly or through a dream, vision, angel, or prophet. At other times, He directed through the ephod, the breastplate of the high priest. "Then David said to Abiathar, the priest, the son of Ahimelek, 'Bring me the ephod.' Abiathar brought it to him, and David inquired of the Lord, 'Shall I pursue . . .'" (1 Sam. 30:7)?

In the New Testament we are instructed to ask for whatever we need in Jesus' name and promised that if we ask, it will be given to us (Matt. 7:7). Between the Word and the Spirit we are abundantly equipped to know. Even Jesus received His Father's guidance through the Scriptures and Spirit (Matt. 4:1–11, Mark 1:35, Luke 5:16).

The End of the Matter

This need to know often comes up in my conversations with my Father. But the personal impasse that stands above all others came just after John's birth (our seventh) as Richard and I discussed the prospect of more Ekhoff children.

I had always wanted a large family. But deeper than a lifetime desire for babies and more babies was a mounting personal conviction that the Lord alone has the right and the wisdom to choose the number of children for each family. Michelle Duggar and I are of one mind. (You may have seen the TV series *19 Kids and Counting*.)

Richard had obviously gone along with my "let God" conviction for a while, but he absolutely drew the line at seven children. I was left in deep confusion because my conviction to obey my husband and my conviction to allow God to determine the number of children contradicted.

I asked for counsel and dug into the bedrock of biblical principle—but Richard remained unmoved by the arguments. Now I desperately needed the Lord's definitive direction. Yet, I dreaded knowing. If the Lord said, "Limit the number of children," my desire would have to be crucified. This option sounded pitilessly painful. If He said, "You may not limit the number of children," Richard and I would remain conflicted. To be honest, although I was willing to hear from the Lord and would certainly obey Him, I believed I was standing in truth and that the Lord would somehow change *Richard* on this issue.

After deliberation and tears, continuing in an attitude of prayer, I felt led to lay this traumatic decision before the Lord as a "fleece" (Judg. 6:1–14)—though this was not my habit, and I'm not recommending this method to others. Didn't the Lord specifically say not to put Him to the "test" (Deut. 6:16, Matt. 4:7)? In His kindness, the Lord Himself provided a conclusive fleece during the very next weeks.

Now it happened that we had just bought a bright red, fifteen-passenger van. It held every person and every person's stuff: car seats, bikes, strollers, backpacks, diaper bags, school projects, snacks, and toys. We loved our rolling family room and christened it "Big Red." Since vanity tags were trendy, I decided to announce something valuable about being a Christian family as we moved about town in our difficult-to-miss vehicle.

A visit to the Division of Motor Vehicles was the first step in the process. With our recently brainstormed list of assertions in seven characters or less, I questioned the employee behind the long desk about which were already in use. Striking several choices, I left with the appropriate form to return by mail.

Later in the day, seated at the kitchen table with the license application before me, I came to the allotted section for clever communiqué. About eight lines had been provided for entries with the instruction to place the most desired ones in the first positions. Upon receiving the application for processing, the unassigned request nearest the top of the list would be granted the requester.

Suddenly, in a revelatory way, I knew (Oh, now I understand!) the form itself was my fleece and one of our favorite choices "7ARROWS" (Psalm 127:4), was the test phrase. The very, very clear number seven would be my way of *knowing* that the Lord had spoken, that we should have seven and only seven children, as unmistakably as writing on a wall—or van.

Carefully, I reviewed the application process thus far: (1) All of my remaining tag ideas appeared to be available. (2) Even if all of my requested tag messages seemed to be available on the DMV printout on this particular date, by the time the form was received for processing at the state office, any of my choices could have been allotted to other drivers. (3) Pending availability, my first entry would automatically be assigned to me.

Based on what I understood, the fleece was laid before the Lord in this way: I purposely placed other tag messages in the first and second choice positions and then added "7ARROWS" in the number three spot, my way of making it harder to receive that particular answer from the Lord.

Then came the anxious wait. Only a few weeks later, an Oklahoma state record of processing speed, I opened the mailbox to find that a package had arrived in the distinct shape of a license plate. Standing transfixed in the driveway, taking a deep breath, and girding courage, I tore into the package. And there it was, embossed black on white—*7ARROWS*.

I now held the Lord's answer in my very hands, but I'd been certain that God wouldn't answer in this direction. As the truth struck, my thought processes froze. Shock washed over me in waves. Tears stung my eyes. For a moment I struggled with such physical weakness that I thought I would faint in the gravel driveway right in front of our mailbox.

I know some will wonder why this decision was so difficult for me. After all, I already had seven—count them—seven children! What could I possibly want with more? To understand, imagine releasing a most cherished dream with no guarantee of its return, not ever. I think that being the mother-of-many was the essence of who I was and laying down the right to this joy required laying all of myself on the altar. It wasn't just the sacrifice of my dream, but the restructure of a strong conviction. It felt like the death of my next child.

In His mercy the Lord added a whole sermon confirmation, so I would be doubly sure. In a Sunday morning service in the next weeks, our pastor preached a sermon based on Exodus 2:1–8, the story of Moses' birth and his narrow escape from death at Pharaoh's decree. I'll never forget her final comments that morning. "As Jochebed set her hand-made basket with its precious occupant into the river's current and watched it float away, she couldn't *know* if he would ever return to her; never-the-less, she released him into the arms of the Lord." Upon hearing these words, in that self-same moment, I fully accepted the required sacrifice, released the dream of another baby into the Spirit's current and watched my basket drift into the faithful arms of the Lord. It was never returned to me.

I grieved for an entire year, but I never doubted that the Lord had chosen the exact number of Ekhoff children. It had been the Lord's right to decide, and He had revealed His choice—I *knew* it. Yes, I mourned, but in hindsight it was a most loving act on my behalf, and I have blessed Him for it.

Sometimes we just don't know how to proceed. In these cases we need the mind of Christ. He knows. And as sons and daughters, we've been given the honor and right to pray that we may also know.

But when the Lord speaks, we receive more than the peace to proceed. The finale of the prayer that must know is simply and profoundly this: We come to *know God* more. He Himself is the dear culmination of every search, the treasure in the field, the pearl of great price (Matt. 13:44–45). In the end to know and enjoy Him in increasing measure is to have every blessing. We walk in the light of Love, and Love is a Person.

Going Deeper
Questions for Small Group Discussion

1. When have you asked Jesus for specific information or next steps? What was your specific question? How did the Lord answer?

2. Have you ever asked the Lord to guide you and when the answer came it was not what you expected or wanted? How did you feel? What was your response?

3. Are you facing a place of indecision? What is a specific question you can hold before the Lord?

The Prayer That Must Wait
Resting in Love

Since ancient times no one has heard, no ear has perceived,
no eye has seen any God besides you,
who acts on behalf of those who wait for him.

Isa. 64:4

My mom Sandra Strange is my mentor and dearest girlfriend. I have learned much by watching her do the Faith very, very well. One of my most cherished adventures in prayer began when she modeled it for me many years ago.

The year 2000 had restructured my mother's life. After discovering that her husband, my stepdad of twenty-two years, was involved in a long-term affair, they had separated in June. In the aftermath, she felt lonelier than at any other time in her life. As her September 1st birthday approached, she found that she was longing to be special to someone. A birthday gift of roses seemed to represent what she had lost, the intimate fellowship of marriage, but there would certainly be no roses this year.

In the meantime Mom had read the testimony of a young woman who had asked the Lord for a specific, personal birthday gift—which He had granted.[12] This was a new thought. Was it really okay to ask God for a birthday gift? Sensing the Lord *inviting* her to do so, she asked Him for roses for her birthday.

September 1ˢᵗ arrived. Anticipating roses at any moment, yet not knowing how they might be delivered, kept her on eager tiptoes. They didn't come when my sister took her out for breakfast, and they didn't come special delivery in the middle of the day.

As the Lord would have it, I flew home on this very day. With 1,100 miles separating her home in Virginia and mine in Oklahoma, I don't think I'd been with Mom on her birthday since I'd left for college 20 years before. When I landed in the early evening, Mom expected that I would disembark with a rose in my hand—I didn't. She was disappointed, but not dismayed, and she didn't even hint about the pending gift.

When we arrived at my mother's home an hour and a half later, it was dark. My sister greeted us on the lighted porch, and we all entered the snug house together. Then surprise, surprise! There on the coffee table was a vase of lovely roses. When I say *lovely*, I minimize the truth. These were no hothouse roses. These were thirty homegrown roses of every extravagant color and fragrance, cut that very afternoon in an old-fashioned southern rose garden, then expertly arranged by someone with talent for such things. When Jesus chooses the gift, it reflects His own taste and is delightfully personal.

While Mom had been at the airport, her thoughtful sister-in-law, knowing nothing of mom's private request, had stopped by with the birthday bouquet. When Mom told us girls the whole story later that evening, I was astounded (See my mother's book *The Lamp, Be Aglow and Burning with the Spirit,* "Roses for My Birthday" for the unabridged rendering). Jesus had given my mother roses for her birthday—a precise request, hand-delivered within the context of twenty-four specific hours? I'd never imagined such a thing was possible. How compassionate is our God! Faith was birthed in me as I became a firsthand witness of the extent of Jesus' kindness. I know now that the Lord flew me to Virginia to see Him give this gift because He knew I would tell you *and He wanted you to know.*

Happy Birthday! Story One

I reflected all year long. By November 2001, the month of my forty-first birthday, I had decided that as God was no respecter of persons, I would also ask Him for a birthday gift.

Asking for a gift from the Lord required much intentional prayer and discernment. I needed to be certain I wanted only what Jesus wanted for me—not without His permission, nor spoiled with greed or selfishness, and most certainly not apart from the Spirit's *wisdom*. That was it! I would ask for a portion of wisdom. Blessed is the daughter who asks for wisdom. Nothing desired compares to it. If anyone lacks wisdom she should ask God who gives generously and it will be given to her (Prov. 3:13–17, James. 1:5).

As my November 28th birthday approached, the fun began. What wisdom would the Lord choose to reveal and how? Would it be a scripture, a sermon, a song? Would His wise instruction be enclosed in a birthday card, or would I receive a phone call? Because I didn't want a kind-intentioned friend to try to fulfill the request, it was held between the Lord and me alone.

On the morning of my birthday it snowed, a gift in itself, as I like a snowy day better than any other. My husband called and offered to take me to lunch, but because of the slippery roads, I ended up parking my car and riding with him to the restaurant.

Almost as soon as I had fastened my seatbelt, I noticed a white plastic cassette tape case between the bucket seats. (This was back in the olden days.)

"What's this?"

Oh, it's just some conference tapes that Ted lent me."

I don't remember anyone lending Richard conference tapes before that time or since. I don't know if he even listened to them. And except for the snow I may have never known he had them. But when I saw the rectangular case, I knew that here was my birthday gift. I just knew.

"Can I take these home and listen to them?"

"Sure."

How sweet to hold in my hand a birthday present picked especially by the Lord on the exact day of my birthday—*no waiting required.*

After lunch, Richard dropped me back at my parked car, and I shoved the first tape into the tape deck as I turned the key in the ignition. When I got home, I listened, took notes, then rewound the tapes and took more notes.

The series was a personal correction for my life. By correction I don't mean that it was upsetting—just resetting. When God corrects me, it's like being guided off in a new direction with His arm around my waist. He confronts with strong *love*.

Over the next year I feasted on the bold statements of my birthday wisdom, comparing them to God's Word and learning to live by them. I couldn't have treasured a birthday present more! (If you are interested, I included some of my notes from this gift at the end of this chapter.) Birthday requests have been a precious part of the conversation between the Lord and me ever since.

Happy Birthday! Story Two

I shared about my 2002 birthday request, "a glimpse of my new house," in an earlier chapter, "Treasure." You will remember that on the very weekend of my birthday, the Lord surprised me with the answer to that request—*again no waiting required.*

Happy Birthday! Story Three

Another year passed. As November approached again, I began the now familiar discernment process of seeking God's face. Psalm 37:4 says, "Take delight in the Lord, and He will give you the desires of your heart." By delighting myself in the character and will of Jesus, I prayed that my will would be tuned and trimmed to His.

I began by discerning where I was and what I needed. An honest evaluation revealed that my life was good. Richard was good and so was his job. My marriage was good. The children? Good. I knew I was doing a good job at what God had called me to do. I had an adequate home and the blueprints for our new home were just being completed. Our family would very likely be moving in the next year or so—very good news. Most importantly, I knew that the Lord is ever Good. I loved Him and knew He loved me.

But if my life was so good, why was I so tired of it? Of late I was tired all the time. I had never been so tired. My last thought when I went to bed was, "Lord, I'm glad I don't have to face tomorrow yet; I have a whole night until it begins," and my first thought on waking was, "How can I face this day?" Inside, where no one could see, silent tears were rusting my soul.

Part of my problem was our home of twenty years. Once charmingly situated in small town Bixby, it was now enveloped in hateful commerce. The depressing view from my front windows consisted of heavy four-lane traffic—the noise was so deafening, we couldn't open windows. A smattering of trash and an assortment of gopher mounds decorated the front lawn. The litter was deposited daily by passing motorists and collected by the children and me when I couldn't stand looking at it any more. The gopher mounds were mowed down with the grass once a week and replaced by the next morning. Longing to see something pretty, I planted flowers. But our dogs dug them up.

Piles of bricks and brick-moving equipment occupied the oily, muddy lot next door, wrapping into a portion of the backyard. Promptly at 4:00 am, the crew began to load brick pallets for daily shipment. The Mack engines fired, and the headlights pierced our bedroom windows.

All of this together bore down on me. My artist's soul was longing for beauty, order, and peace, but there was no oasis upon which to rest my gaze.

For exercise and time alone to think a few thoughts together, I devised a footpath that passed through the breezeway connecting our house and garage, wound round the garage, and arrived full circle at the breezeway again. The children, who were usually playing in the yard at this time of day, could see me and call to me if needed.

One November afternoon as I plodded my path like a tethered pony, I thought to myself, "I feel like I am wearing a backpack filled with these bricks. My life is too heavy for me. If someone would just take a few bricks out of my backpack, I could stand up straight." And there was my birthday request. I knew because the Holy Spirit immediately confirmed it.

So in the next breath I asked, "Lord, will you take some of the bricks out of my backpack, so I can stand up straight?" Though I had the firm conviction that the Lord was leading me to ask, truthfully, I couldn't imagine how even He could help me. I was that depleted.

Some of you have waited patiently for me to share how this story illustrates the prayer that must wait and at long last I come to the point. On this birthday I eagerly, desperately waited for the lightening of my load, the miracle of strength to go on. A week passed, a month, two, three, and nothing changed. In the past the Lord had answered my requests immediately—within a day or two of my exact birthdate. But this time, there was no answer.

Eventually, the green of buds and shoots announced spring. One warm afternoon I decided to enjoy a walk on my pony path. Plod, plod, plod. Tired, tired, tired. Nothing had changed. The day's offering of trash was blowing across the lawn, the traffic was particularly deafening, and the brickyard especially oily and muddy.

In that moment I reached a breaking point. "Lord, I can't go on! I asked You to lighten my load. Why have You forgotten me?" Without a moment's pause, the Lord replied. "Some gifts take an entire year to give!" He was smiling as He said it, even suppressing a giggle. Does God laugh? He did then.

Somehow His explanation sparked hope. "Hope deferred makes the heart sick" (Prov. 13:12), but hope kindled sustains. I mentally calculated the months that would complete the full year. There were eight months until my next birthday. I determined that if God helped me, I could do almost anything for eight months, so I set my gaze and I plodded on: "But if we hope for what we do not yet have, we wait for it patiently" (Rom. 8:25).

By the second week of November 2003, our new house was finished, and we had moved. This in itself was a relief, but I was still internally dull with increasing pain in my joints and muscles. I felt adrift in a dense fog.

In exasperation and with my husband's strong encouragement, I went to see our family doctor. After listening quietly, he suggested that I was suffering from fibromyalgia (I already suspected this from a previous diagnosis) and depression, and since the research to date found antidepressants to be of benefit to both, he suggested I might try one.

I was aggravated. I didn't need far-fetched ideas about my mental health, and I certainly didn't need an antidepressant. The very idea! I said something rather kinder to my doctor, who was also a family friend. He countered that I was prejudiced against anti-depression medication. Was I? He assured me that I wouldn't have to take much to be able to tell if it would help. So grudgingly I filled the prescription and began with a half a tablet the next morning.

I will never forget the surprise breakthrough about two weeks later. The children were gathered in the kitchen and I was rocking in the red rocker when one of them said something funny, and I laughed aloud. Someone commented incredulously, "Mom, did *you* just laugh?" I thought for a moment. When was the last time I had laughed? I couldn't even remember. I replied, "I think I did!"

With a start I realized that the year was over, and I had just received the final installment of my birthday present. Just as the Lord had said, it had taken a whole year for us to build and move. It had taken a whole year of tolerating oppression and pain to humble myself and ask for help. It had taken a whole year to admit that I was suffering from depression. The Lord's gift had been well worth the wait. How I praised Him in that moment, and now as I write this testimony, His Goodness washes over me again.

I weaned myself off of the depression meds within three months, and that was all the boost I needed to break the stronghold of depression. Best of all, in this year of waiting, the Lord weaned me from the need for immediately answered prayer. Now I wait patiently, confidently without having to be reminded to wait (most of the time) and am content.

The Prayer That Must Wait in Practice

Those who desire sweeter, deeper conversations with the Father must learn to rest in trust—trust in His character, wisdom, sovereignty, will, and timing. "Yet the Lord longs to be gracious to you; therefore he will rise up to show you compassion. For the Lord is a God of justice. Blessed are all who wait for him" (Isa. 30:18)

The following are some principles of the prayer that must wait in practice. They are the sure paths to the mature conversational prayer that we all want, but are sometimes too impatient to fully realize.

Discerning God's Heart

If I could, I would announce this first principle with fanfare and a red carpet. This advice can't be over emphasized and HERE IT IS: Wait to know God's heart before making a petition. In this discernment phase we wait for the Lord to reveal what to ask. Waiting demonstrates our submission and deference to His will. We need His wisdom to ask aright.

When the disciples asked Jesus to teach them to pray, He taught them to say "Your kingdom come, your will be done, on earth as it is in Heaven" (Matt. 6:10). In like manner we can initiate petition by asking Jesus to teach us to pray. Then as He reveals His will on earth as it is in Heaven, we are rightfully positioned to make a request based on His delight. Asking in this way simultaneously fulfills the desire of our hearts (Ps. 37:4).

This one practice has revolutionized my prayer life. I highly recommend the joys of praying God's will back to Him. In this relational precursor, we await the coming of the Lord as Wonderful Counselor.

On occasion I add fasting to discernment. Fasting can fine-tune our ability to hear the Lord's voice. To be honest, my flesh hates fasting, but I have never, ever been sorry I did it.

Focusing on the Priority

Sometimes we want the answer to our prayer so much that we fixate on the answer instead of the Lord, Who *is* the Answer.

- "Lord, *I wait for you;* you will answer, Lord my God" (Ps. 38:15, emphasis mine).
- "Yes, Lord, walking in the way of your laws, *we wait for you;* your name and renown are the desire of our hearts" (Isa. 26:8, emphasis mine).
- *"I waited patiently for the Lord;* he turned to me and heard my cry" (Ps. 40:1, emphasis mine).

We wait for a Person, then His answer.

Transitioning in the Liminal Place

The prayer that must wait is the liminal place between the request and the answer. Liminal means the transitional stage, occupying a position on both sides of a threshold.

"Now faith is confidence in what we hope for and assurance about what we do not see" (Heb. 11:1). The request, or "what we hope for," is the initial position in prayer. The answer, "what we do not see" is somewhere in our future. Between these two footholds, faith bonds the known request with the unrealized answer. In this sense we have a foothold in both positions as we transition from the old to the new.

When I accused the Lord of forgetting me, I think He laughed because He was personally overseeing the transition between my request and His answer and holding me in the midst of it. In the uncertainty of the liminal place, Jesus assures us that we are His, and He is ours. Our Father is Jehovah Jireh, The Lord will Provide. What comfort.

Waiting in Hope

Some Hebrew words translated wait or hope are interchangeable. Consider Psalm 130:5: "I *wait* (Heb. qavah—wait, look for, hope, expect) for the Lord, my whole being *waits* (qavah), and in his word I put my *hope*" (Heb. yachal—wait, hope, expect). Italics here are my addition. So Psalm 130:5 could read, "I wait and hope for the Lord, my whole being waits and hopes, and in his word I wait and hope."

When I lost hope, my waiting lost its buoyancy, which almost led to despair. When the Lord restored my hope, I was able to wait many months for His timely answer.

Hope waits, and waiting hopes. In tandem they produce strength and power. "But those who wait for the Lord [who expect, look for, and hope in Him] shall change and renew their strength and power . . . They shall run and not be weary, they shall walk and not faint or become tired" (Isa. 40:31 AMPC).

Understanding Seasons

Sometimes the need to wait has everything to do with seasons. It's not always time to receive. "There is a time for everything and a season for every activity under the Heavens" (Eccles. 3:1).

There was a reason I had to wait a whole year for my "backpack to be lightened." The season for building a new house had to precede the season for living in it. The season for humbling myself had to precede the season for healing.

"Be patient, then, brothers and sisters, until the Lord's coming. See how the farmer waits for the land to yield its valuable crop, patiently waiting for the autumn and spring rains. You too, be patient and stand firm, because the Lord's coming is near" (James 5:7–8). I think James may be referring to Jesus's second coming, but this passage could also be interpreted as the Lord's coming intervention in our situation. The due season will surely come, but not until its time. Wait for it.

Valuing the Process

The prayer that must wait creates perseverance and perseverance is priceless. Those who long to be mature and complete must trudge the steep and winding stairs that produce it. We can't be mature and complete without the heart-strengthening strain of waiting.

James goes so far as to say that this stressful process should be celebrated! The more difficulty endured now, the more strength to endure later. "You know that the testing of your faith produces perseverance. Let perseverance finish its work so that you may be mature and complete, not lacking anything" (James. 1:3–4).

We may scorn the refining stress of perseverance in the moment. But later we wouldn't take anything for what we've gained. Thank you, Father, for not giving us the option to sidestep the process.

An Invitation to Ask

Corrie ten Boom once wrote, "Some have been strengthened by my telling of small and large miracles God did in my life and dare now bring their own difficulties to Him."[13] That is the purpose of this chapter. I hope that reading my little tales of birthday surprises will encourage you to discern and ask for them. Yes, it is within the will of God to discern what He is poised to give us—even if it is something personal—and ask Him for it. He is so much more than expected, and His gifts are like Him.

After many years of persevering through, I now know that some gifts take *longer* than a year to give—some take a lifetime. Some are even sealed for future generations. That means that people I may never know on earth will receive the answers to my prayers. Glory! Meditating on the heady responsibility and power of the prayer that must wait could change the way we pray! As we wait for the answer to our prayers, we have the luxury of resting in Love, and Love is a Person.

Going Deeper
Questions for Small Group Discussion

1. If you could ask the Lord for anything, what would you ask for?

2. When have you wanted to pray but didn't know what to pray for? Have you ever waited before the Lord until He revealed His direction for prayer, then prayed according to His will? What was the outcome?

3. When did the *process* bless you more than the *culmination* of prayer? Which experiences in your life have required the most perseverance? How has the strength you gained benefitted you or those you love?

4. Describe a personal liminal place between your petition and God's answer. How did you feel as you waited in faith?

5. Share about a time when your hope dissipated. How is waiting with hope different than waiting without it?

6. There is a time for everything (Eccles. 3:1). Look back over the seasons of your life. Share about a transition season, a frustrating season, a joyous season, a grief-filled season. How did they begin and end? What did you learn from these experiences?

Wisdom for My Birthday[14]

These are my dear wisdom nuggets and corrections from my birthday gift, year one. If Jesus is reading this to you in heaven, Dr. Wells, thank you for wrapping my birthday gift in your hard-won experience.

- *"If you can be offended, you deserve to be."* This was offensive the first time I heard it! But now I understand that God doesn't cross His arms and pout. I was too easily offended and didn't mind showing it. I needed to grow up.

- *"Truth is purchased at a counter that God sets up, when I exchange my will for His will."* I loved truth but had never equated its acquisition to the relinquishment of my will.

- *"Some attitudes make us 'unsafe' for God to be willing to place the mentoring of others into our hands."* It has taken many years for the Lord to knead this truth into my life. To my sorrow I had many *unsafe* attitudes. I was quick to make judgments and hold grudges. I was eager to fix people so they would be pleasing to me and slow to release people into the freedom of the Lord. I wasn't transparent about my personal faults and failures, so people were afraid to be honest with me about theirs. This was wisdom to grow on.

- *God is not willing to share His glory.* Most people already know this, but I didn't. I thought He shared His glory with His people—specifically me. I had confused seeing, reflecting, enjoying, and worshipping the Lord of glory with possessing His glory.

- *Humility is crucial.* Over the next few years the Lord drafted me into a humility boot camp that taught me more than I thought I needed to learn about humility—to my great benefit.

The Prayer That Must Win
Standing in Love

"Don't be afraid of them.
Remember the Lord, who is great and awesome,
and fight for your families, your sons and your daughters,
your wives and your homes."
Neh. 4:14

Deliver us from evil;
for yours is the Kingdom and the power and the glory forever. Amen
The Lord's Prayer, Matt. 6:13

On a good day, parenting is sweet beyond describing, and on a routine day, the happy motivation to be persistent and faithful. But in turbulent seasons, parenting is the most stretching and vulnerable of charges. It was a season like the later when the Lord revealed His empathy with my parenting pain, and His ability to carry my family through.

In mid-January 2008, I woke from an uneasy sleep about 4:30 a.m. My *first* conscious thought was that my *last* conscious thought had been wrenching. Then I remembered yesterday's disclosure: two Ekhoff children had been involved in reprehensible behavior while on my watch. (I will not share the offense, as this testimony is more about God's good word to me than this particular sin.) Remembering the incident I felt sorrow billow in again, shadowed by shame.

Sleep dispelled, I slipped to the family room, my place for early morning counsels with the Lord. Pulling a chair close to the gas fireplace flames, tucking my feet for warmth, and opening my Bible on the ample arm of the chair, I began an earnest search for the Lord—His voice, His comfort, His counsel.

I knew that somewhere in the margins I had written little notes beside verses that the Lord had indicated were for my children, promises I'd made to Him and promises He'd made to me. This morning I was yearning for these in particular:

- "These commandments I give you today are to be upon your hearts. Impress them on your children. Talk about them when you sit at home and when you walk along the road, when you lie down and when you get up. Tie them as symbols on your hands and bind them on your foreheads. Write them on the doorframes of your houses and on your gates" (Deut. 6:6–9). I'd written here, "Our homeschool foundation" and committed to live it.

- "I prayed for this child, and the Lord has granted me what I asked of Him. So now I give him to the Lord. For his whole life he will be given over to the Lord (I Sam. 1:27–28). Like Hannah, I had prayed for each child. I knew that my children were gifts, and I'd given them back to the Lord for their whole lives.

- "Praise the Lord. Blessed are those who fear the Lord, who find great delight in His commands. Their children will be mighty in the land; the generation of the upright will be blessed" (Ps. 112:1–2). I believed that to be "blessed" meant that our family would receive the rewards of obeying God's commands. But how could the Ekhoff family be characterized by obedience when our bent to sin was so strong? The stink of sin was especially before me this morning. I was ashamed of my distractions and blamed myself. I was shocked by what my children could be tempted to do. Where had God been in our weakness?

As I clutched at these scriptures, a prayer formed—not a tender, humble prayer—a hot, accusing prayer: "You promised! You promised! YOU PROMISED!" Between spitting accusations at God and begging forgiveness, I sobbed. For two hours I raged and repented until the inner storm quelled. As there was nothing more to say, I sat quietly and waited for the voice of the Lord. But though I anticipated in faith, there was no word from Him. In the ensuing silence, I felt betrayed.

You must be wondering at my shallowness. Why didn't I heed the promises I'd just read? Where was my faith? But remember our conversation with our Father is relational. I wanted more than verses, I wanted to be immersed in His comfort. I wanted His assurance that all was forgiven. I needed specific instruction for the present crisis. He is able and willing to be Wonderful Counselor, Mighty God, Prince of Peace (Isa. 9:6).

By 7:30 a.m., I began to hear footfall and voices above me. The children would soon tumble down for breakfast and the start of our school day. Taking a deep breath, I resolved to pull myself together. I replaced the chair, put my Bible away, switched off the light, and headed to the kitchen where I busied about with breakfast preparations. Still needing to dress for the day, about 7:45 I started back through the family room—but came to a full stop mid-step.

Now on the opposite family room wall I had arranged a decorative collage above the sofa. The bottom row consisted of three shadow boxes side-by-side filled with snapshots of my children. Above these was a 6 x 40" wooden plaque. On this I had hand-lettered a verse in pine green paint: "Behold, children are an heritage from the Lord" (Ps. 127:3, my own combination of the AMP and KJV). Above the plaque were two small woodcarvings, and atop these a small wreath.

I had grown past noticing anything on this wall unless the pictures were askew, but this morning I stared unblinking across the semi-dark room. Here's why: The plaque was highlighted in white light. Not precisely framed—but trust me—framed more than enough to make a holy impression.

As I stood transfixed and confused, my first thought was to question if it was really light, then to marvel at how the light accented only the plaque and its message as if designed to do so. The old adage, "Read the writing on the wall," came to mind. Then I seriously considered the possibility of something supernatural. Could it be that God had literally highlighted this particular message in answer to my agonized prayer?

I flew across the room and stepped up onto the sofa for a closer look. Extending my hand high above my head and turning round and round, I searched for an explainable light source. As it turned out, the rising sun was just breaking over the roofs of our neighbors' homes to the east and streaming through the transom window above our front door. The shape of the transom happened to be similar to the shape of the plaque.

Then my mind went a whirling: Such a God! Such a comforting passage for my present situation! Such a gracious, timely answer to my angry prayer! After a few moments of wonder and praise, I headed down the hall to my bedroom. As I did, like Mary, I treasured up all these things and pondered them in my heart (Luke 2:19). I think our Father enjoys surprises that undo us.

Taking a picture didn't enter my mind until mid-day, but next morning I was on hand at 7:45 a.m. to see what I could discover about the transom-framed sunlight and its relationship with the family room wall, and you can bet I had my camera in my hand. But the next morning was overcast, so was the next, and the next. On Friday morning I got my picture.

A Calculation

Do these kinds of answers to prayer happen at random, or does God plan them? Let's do a little math to calculate the probability of my seeing a plaque displaying a case-specific, sunlit message on the very morning I desperately needed comfort from my Father. If you like math, you'll love this.

To establish this calculation I think we must begin with Properties One and Two: (1) Our Good God cares deeply (1 Pet. 5:7). He cared that my children and I would fall and that I would be heartbroken. (2) He foreknows (Ps. 139:4). He knew the day and hour I would call to Him.

Now, we can deduce possible factors. First, let's estimate the number of days per year that the sun rises at an angle that would light the plaque in a compelling way, taking into account it would be in this position twice because of summer and winter solstice. By my observations the "lighted plaque" position is compelling for barely 7 days in each solstice, making the number of days that the plaque would have had enough sunlight to make me stop and say, "Wow! That must be God!" no more than 14 days out of 365.

Next, let's calculate the number of sunny days to cloudy days in January in my part of the world. According to Oklahoma weather records, the ratio of the number of sunny/partly sunny days to cloudy days is 17 out of 31 in the month of January. I've been generous here because there are only 10 sunny days, and not all partly sunny days would light the plaque.

Now let's consider the number of minutes per day that the sunlight reaches and holds this arresting position over the plaque. I have observed that this measurement is a maximum of five minutes out of the 24-hour day.

Bear with me—are we having fun yet? This is how those numbers compute:

$$14/365 \text{ (days of the year that the transom shaped sunlight is superimposed on the plaque)}$$
$$\text{x } 17/31 \text{ (sunny/partly sunny days in the month of January in Oklahoma)}$$
$$\text{x } 5/(60 \text{ min. x } 24 \text{ hrs.) that the plaque is lit in such a way to lock my attention on its message}$$
$$= .03835 \text{ x } .54838 \text{ x } .00347$$
$$= .000073 \text{ or } 73/1,000,000$$
$$= 1/13,697$$

That's about a 1 in 13,700 chance that I would see the lighted plaque on this particular morning.

But these are only the numbers that can be calculated. Not all of the factors are quantifiable:

- The angle of my home on the surface of the earth in relation to the rising sun
- The position and shape of the transom window
- The exact placement of the plaque on the wall
- The arbitrary electric lighting in my family room, which could obscure the impact of the sunlight

- The direct correlation between the meaning of the verse and my situation as compared to the myriad of messages that could have been painted on the plaque
- The fact that I had chosen the passage and painted it myself, which adds meaning to me, and the word *Behold* (see, observe, witness), which prefaces the verse
- That I would enter the family room from the kitchen at this exact time of day providing the best chance to see the north wall
- The uncertainty of my looking up or paying attention in my sleep deprived, sorrowful, and hurried passage through the family room
- And even the chance that I might reject the direct answer to my prayer as mere happenstance

These cannot be mathematically understood.

It's my opinion that these additional factors are more viable, though not quantifiable, and if calculated would certainly put this number in the range of impossibility. In my book that constitutes a miracle, and since I am honored to be the author of this book, I will refer to this experience as "the miracle of the plaque."

Why did the Lord go to so much trouble? I believe it was partly for me and partly for you. A fight is on for those we love, and He wants you and me to know that our children (and all those who are dear to us) are *His* heritage gifted as *our* heritage. That means my lit plaque is your lit plaque. "Whoever fears the Lord has a secure fortress, and for their children it will be a refuge" (Prov. 14:26).

The Nature of the Battle

The prayer that must win is a strong, animated conversation with God on behalf of those He has entrusted to us: our spouse, children, parents, and friends. In intercession it can even include people we have never met. He loves them. We love them. Together we will fight for them.

On the morning that I wept before the Lord for two hours, I knew very little about the prayer that must win. My family hadn't been openly tested for some time. I'd forgotten that satan wants to destroy us, and our sin nature is capable of detestable behaviors. I was dozing at my post.

Since then the Lord has unveiled His arsenal for warfare and trained my hands "for the bow" as I contend for those I love. "It is God who arms me with strength and keeps my way secure . . . He trains my hands for battle; my arms can bend a bow of bronze. You make your saving help my shield, and your right hand sustains me; your help has made me great" (Ps. 18:32–35).

I understand that "spiritual warfare" is controversial in some Christian circles, but this chapter is not about taking on satan and his demons as if Jesus is not all in all. I pray you'll find my story user friendly and not overtly edgy. But before that, let's look at what we're up against. What is the root of evil?

The Two Revolts

Edith Schaeffer, author and co-founder of L'Abri Fellowship International, expertly describes the cosmic clash between good and evil in this way: There has been a revolt in the unseen (spiritual) and the seen (physical) portions of creation, that is the heavens and the earth. These revolts were against the character of God. The revolt in heaven resulted in the expulsion of lucifer (satan) and one third of the angels, who now make war against the Most High, His angels, and His people. The revolt on earth resulted in Adam and Eve's expulsion from the Garden of Eden and the physical and spiritual death of Adam's race—that's you and me.

These two revolts are the historical reality of our moral dilemma. Something is wrong in the world. Only those who hold a worldview tainted by naturalism look on in amazement. (Naturalism is the philosophical view, which rejects all supernatural or spiritual explanations for the realities of the natural world.) Those who hold a Christian worldview know the truth about the revolts and their remedy. The Second Adam, Jesus, broke the power of the revolt on both fronts, in heaven and on earth (Matt. 28:18). The historical death and resurrection of Jesus Messiah are the power and glory of the prayer that must win.[15]

Who is the Enemy?

Though we perpetrate evil by participation, *we* are not the enemy. The Scriptures are clear concerning the identity of the enemies of God and man. They are the evil directed from without—satan and his demons, and the evil birthed from within—our sin nature.

The battle *without* is not waged against flesh and blood people, "but against the rulers, against the authorities, against the powers of this dark world and against the spiritual forces of evil in the heavenly realms" (Eph. 6:12). We must never forget that our spiritual enemy is very real. He hates each of us. He moves in half-truths and deception. He and his cohorts detest light, life, love, and truth and persistently strike to kill, steal, and destroy. Yet the victory is strong and sure. "We are more than conquerors through him who loved us. [We are] convinced that neither death nor life, neither angels nor demons, neither the present nor the future, nor any powers, neither height nor depth, nor anything else in all creation, will be able to separate us from the love of God that is in Christ Jesus our Lord" (Rom. 8:37–39).

The battle *within* is waged against our inborn fallen nature or the natural man. This evil originates in our hearts then infiltrates our thoughts, words, and actions. The Apostle Paul explains that our fallen nature wages war against the character of God and makes us a prisoner to sin, but Jesus has decisively rescued us from this body that is subject to spiritual and physical death (Rom. 7:21–24). "Thanks be to God, who delivers me through Jesus Christ our Lord" (Rom. 7:25).

The Battle is the Lord's

Each person—no exceptions—must face these two enemies. There is no place to hide. But our strong Savior's authoritative love infinitely exceeds our enemies' hatred (1 John 4:4), and His blood cleanses every sin (Eph. 2:13). He is our Rock, Fortress, Deliverer, High Tower, Shield, and Refuge (Ps. 18:2; 41:2; 59:1, 9; Ps. 91:4). In the DVD production *Furious Love, This Time Love Fights Back*, Darren Wilson[16] concludes, "The war has brought us pain, fear, doubt, and abuse. But there is One who fights for us still, One who stands against the darkness. He rides a white horse and carries a sword in his hand. He is our Defender, our God, our Father." The prayer that must win is launched in the knowledge that the Lord, who is victor at all times, ultimately wins all battles against His character. It was not by their sword that they won the land, nor did their arm bring them victory; it was your right hand, your arm, and the light of your face, for you loved them" (Ps 44:3).

The Stance

The battle is the Lord's, but that doesn't mean we have no part in it. We exercise our authority to say, "Yes!" to the movement of the Holy Spirit and, "No!" to satan's schemes. We act on His instructions. We are conduits of His love. We stand in faith.

I'd like to illustrate the stance of the prayer that must win with one of the final scenes of the movie *Prince Caspian*.[17] The army of King Miraz, Narnia's enemy, is advancing on the town of Beruna. To reach the city they must cross the Ford of Beruna by way of a wooden bridge, but a single, defiant combatant holds a position on the opposite side. Lucy, a child of eleven or twelve, faces the advancing army with an unsheathed four-inch blade. Aslan, who represents Jesus, approaches and stands beside her. Miraz is momentarily taken aback by their audacity, but what is a mere child and a lion before the power of His army? With a rush the army advances. The astute viewer looks on knowing that Miraz is doomed. Indeed the army is swept away when Aslan suddenly unleashes the river—and Lucy stands as witness and victor.

Yes, we take a position with a spiritual weapon in hand (see the weapons of our arsenal below), but it would be laughable to think that our strength or wisdom brings the victory any more than Lucy's blade prevented Miraz's advance. You [Lord] armed me with strength for battle; You humbled my adversaries before me (Ps. 18:39).

Whether we see the complete victory in our lifetime or wait for it to be unveiled when the final judgments and recompenses are made at the end of the age, we can remain uncompromised because He is uncompromised, and we are in Him. "Hear, Israel: Today you are going into battle against your enemies. Do not be fainthearted or afraid; do not panic or be terrified by them. For the Lord your God is the one who goes with you to fight for you against your enemies to give you victory" (Deut. 20:3–4).

Our Arsenal

Wielding the prayer that must win requires choosing divine weapons for warfare, and discernment is always a part of the choosing. "For though we live in the world, we do not wage war as the world does. Our weapons are not the weapons of this world. On the contrary, they have divine power to demolish strongholds" (2 Cor. 10:3–4). When we face our spiritual enemy, whether the attack is against us personally or those we love, we can ask the Holy Spirit to reveal the most advantageous weapon and act on His direction. Jesus' weapons work because they reflect His Person and wield His Power.

- *Using the authority of the Name*—"Lord, even the demons submit to us in your name" (Luke 10:17).
- *Applying Jesus' blood and the word of our testimony*—"They triumphed over him by the blood of the Lamb and by the word of their testimony; they did not love their lives so much as to shrink from death" (Rev. 12:11).
- *Intercession*—"I urge, then, first of all, that petitions, prayers, intercession and thanksgiving be made for all people . . ." (1 Tim. 2:1).
- *Worship*—"Worship the Lord your God; it is he who will deliver you from the hand of all your enemies" (2 Kings 17:39).
- *Giving thanks, praying continually and rejoicing in all circumstances*—"Rejoice always, pray continually, give thanks in all circumstances; for this is God's will for you in Christ Jesus" (1 Thess. 5:16–18). You will remember that my mother was given this scripture in her battle with my dad's alcoholism and the joyous victory that was hers.
- *Holding to truth*—"[satan] was a murderer from the beginning, not holding to the truth, for there is no truth in him. When he lies, he speaks his native language, for he is a liar and the father of lies" (John 8:44b). "If you hold to my teaching, you are really my disciples. Then you will know the truth, and the truth will set you free" (John 8:31b–32).
- *Goodness*—"Do not be overcome by evil, but overcome evil with good" (Rom 12:21).

- *Weakness*—"But he said to me, 'My grace is sufficient for you, for my power is made perfect in weakness.' Therefore I will boast all the more gladly about my weaknesses, so that Christ's power may rest on me. That is why, for Christ's sake, I delight in weaknesses, in insults, in hardships, in persecutions, in difficulties. For when I am weak, then I am strong" (2 Cor. 12:9–10).

- *Forgiveness*—"Bear with each other and forgive one another if any of you has a grievance against someone. Forgive as the Lord forgave you" (Col. 3:13).

- *Standing*—"Therefore put on the full armor of God, so that when the day of evil comes, you may be able to stand your ground, and after you have done everything, to stand. Stand firm then, with the belt of truth buckled around your waist, with the breastplate of righteousness in place, and with your feet fitted with the readiness that comes from the gospel of peace" (Eph. 6:13–15).

- *Faith*—"In addition to all this, take up the shield of faith, with which you can extinguish all the flaming arrows of the evil one" (Eph. 6:16). "For everyone born of God overcomes the world. This is the victory that has overcome the world, even our faith" (1 John 5:4).

- *Support*—"So Joshua fought the Amalekites as Moses had ordered, and Moses, Aaron and Hur went to the top of the hill. As long as Moses held up his hands, the Israelites were winning, but whenever he lowered his hands, the Amalekites were winning. When Moses' hands grew tired, they took a stone and put it under him and he sat on it. Aaron and Hur held his hands up—one on one side, one on the other—so that his hands remained steady till sunset. So Joshua overcame the Amalekite army with the sword" (Ex. 17:10–13). "Therefore encourage one another and build each other up, just as in fact you are doing" (1 Thess. 5:11).

- *Sacrificial Love*—"This is how we know what love is: Jesus Christ laid down his life for us. And we ought to lay down our lives for our brothers and sisters" (1 John 3:16). "Greater love has no one than this: to lay down one's life for one's friends" (John 15:13). "Love covers over a multitude of sins"

(1 Pet. 4:8b). Jesus demonstrated by his life and death that there is no love without sacrifice. Sacrifice means relinquishing our rights and will. It means relinquishing those we love into the hands of God. It means suffering on their behalf. Sacrificial love dissolves enemy tactics and wins by losing. Love never fails. Dutch missionary and pastor, Jan Sjoerd Pasterkamp witnesses to the power of love: "I did my thesis on spiritual warfare . . . and I have come to the conclusion after a long time of study that the greatest weapon we have against the devil is love. When God wanted to redeem a world that had come into the hands of satan . . . He used love." [18]

- *Other powerful weapons*—unity, mercy, rest, empathy, peace, humility, tough love, and preaching and acting on the Word. No doubt you can think of many others. Unsheathed at the Spirit's command, these weapons are a formidable arsenal indeed!

Prepared to Win

Following the miracle of the plaque in 2008, I enjoyed a time of peace. Then the Lord prophetically prepared me for the tumultuous season ahead. In February 2010, I was remembering the miracle of the plaque—I don't remember why it had come to mind this particular morning—when the Lord spoke. "You have not fully understood the significance of this verse and I want you to. I am making a *covenant* with you concerning your children that cannot be broken. Your children are My heritage."

Later that month He adjusted my understanding of parenting. A close friend and I were praying for our husbands and children when the Holy Spirit began to speak. The physical words were mine, but even as I articulated them, I knew the Lord was using my voice to speak them back to me. He said, "You are attributing the success or failure of your family to your parenting skills, and that is presumption. I do the core work of parenting and provide grace when you make mistakes. To illustrate, He showed me a hand in a glove. I knew by the Spirit that the hand was the Lord's and my intentional parenting merely a glove—an instrument of His will. He closed the revelation by saying, "It is finished." I was given understanding as He made this statement. From the Father's eternal perspective, my parenting is complete. All the days of my children's lives are fully known from beginning to end.

I'd never been the vessel of prophetic prayer quite like this before and was surprised by the Father's perspective. Of course, I wrote these impressions in my journal for safekeeping—and it was a good thing I did. My journal is beside me now, and as I turn the page, the very next entry is titled, "And Now All Hell Breaks Loose!"

The "hell" was unleashed over months into years as several of our children suffered blow after blow from the enemy without and the enemy within. I know you'll agree that our most painful experiences are when our children are broken before our eyes. Though I'm not at liberty to share the details of the myriad of struggles and the people involved in this context, I will testify to some hard won lessons in hopes that they will shout encouragement as you fight the good fight for your loved ones.

High Alert

The prayer that must win is a red alert prayer on two fronts. Chiefly, we are attentive for the Lord's voice and His movement in our relationships and circumstances. We're also vigilant to enemy infiltration.

The Lord's Movement

When my heart was frozen with fear for my children, I found in Jesus everything I needed to battle for them. He led me beside still waters, he restored my soul. Even when I walked through the valley of the shadow of death, I was not alone. His goodness and mercy pursued us all (Ps. 23). Jesus bade me soak in His presence (the weapon of rest), groan in prayer at night (the weapon of intercession), and bathe my mind in worship choruses in my afternoon walks in the park (the weapon of worship). As I unsheathed these weapons in quiet and trust, the Spirit provided instruction for my next steps, so I was never without counsel.

On several early mornings just as I was waking, the Holy Spirit prompted me to write a long letter or buy a thoughtful gift (weapons of goodness). Then I set other responsibilities aside to discharge His brilliant ideas.

Sometimes the Lord simply wanted me to journal and meditate. In one journal exercise the Holy Spirit led me to confront my self-talk by making a list of everything I'd done well as a parent, then list my failures (the weapon of truth). I was amazed to find I had been a pretty good parent and thanked Him for this bit of good news! I had several areas that needed improvement and set to work making these lifestyle changes. Some mistakes were beyond my ability to change, and I had to lean into God my strength (the weapon of weakness). I asked the Lord for forgiveness and forgave myself. I released those who had sinned against me (the weapon of forgiveness).

When tension mounted, Richard and I locked arms, so the pressure wouldn't pry us apart. Sometimes we prayed in each other's arms. Richard's prayers carried weight. As the spiritual head of our home, I could feel the atmosphere change when he set the situation before the Lord. When I was atremble and confused, he was strong and decisive. When he was rigid and narrow, I brought flexibility and perspective. Yes, tension hammered at our marriage, but we were by no means crushed; we were struck down, but never destroyed (2 Cor. 4:7–8). Through years of uncharted chaos, my husband protected our children and me as he submitted himself to God (the weapon of unity). Thanks be to God!

Prompted by the Lord, I humbled myself (the weapon of humility) and called on a few select family and friends for prayer, advice, and comfort (the weapon of support). These saints heard my transparent confessions and kept the confidence. How gentle they were in my hour of raw pain. The Lord heard and answered their prayers.

Perhaps harder than doing something was waiting submitted and prepared (the weapon of standing). The Spirit often required that I know things, but not speak of them to anyone but Himself. A few times He required me to use His revelation to confront (the weapon of tough love).

In these years I surrendered my children into the arms of the Lord and stepped away, not knowing what would happen. My rights and expectations had to be relinquished. I sometimes bore the brunt of my children's bad choices (weapons of sacrificial love). These hurt! But the Lord held me secure.

One night in particular I was at my end—gut-level distraught. At bedtime I told the Lord to wake me in the middle of the night, and when He did, I was going to wrestle Him to the ground—if you can believe it—this sounded like a reasonable idea to me. (You will remember that Jacob wrestled the Lord all night in Gen. 32.)

When I woke in the wee hours, I stormed to the family room and vehemently presented my case against God, listing His negligent oversights. The audacity! But when I stood facing Him in the ensuing calm, He spoke decisively, "The crisis is over," and put months of terror to flight. Looking back, He was right, the crisis was over.

The enemy's Movement

The second part of the prayer that must win involves alert attention to enemy movement. I liken this part of the battle to playing high-stakes poker. Empowered by the Spirit, I watched for clues as "cards" were laid face up—reactions, body language, words, actions, attitudes, social media, stressed relationships. With attention to these, I could spiritually discern the concealed cards— the root issues and hidden pain that drove these actions. When I heeded the clues, I had good information about enemy tactics. I learned that he is characterized by overplaying his hand and if I don't panic, I can take the trick.

I often announced the unveiled schemes to my Father and used His authority. "NO! Not on my watch. I take authority in JESUS' NAME! I belong to the Lord and these children are given over to Him; you can't have them! I see your plan. Get out in Jesus' name!" Sometimes when alone, I stood on the sofa with fists raised for emphasis. That wasn't necessary of course, since Jesus' name is completely effective without the drama—but it made me feel better.

Terrible and Beautiful

I need to be clear here. The prayer that must win is not a tidy process. I was a mess. I was shell-shocked. I cried a lot. I was clumsy with my weapons. I missed my cues and took hairpin turns to circle back. I did not win every battle and everything did not end happily ever after. But I did experience intimacy with God and saw Him do miraculous things. Even now, scenes from this period punctuate Bible verses and worship choruses—I know they are true because I lived them. The Lord revealed Himself in my battle, and He will reveal Himself in yours as well.

The prayer that must win is both terrible and beautiful. It is terrible because facing sin and pain is shocking, even horrific. But it is also intrinsically beautiful, for as we battle for love's sake we are never alone. We take our stand in Love, and Love is a Person.

Who is this coming from Edom, from Bozrah,
with his garments stained crimson?
Who is this, robed in splendor, striding forward in the greatness of his strength?
"It is I, proclaiming victory, mighty to save."
Isa. 63:1

Going Deeper
Questions for Small Group Discussion

1. The enemy is never a person. Have you ever struggled loving the person and hating the sin? In what ways did you demonstrate love?

2. Which spiritual weapons have you wielded? Which ones would you like to try?

3. Some victories are not fully realized in this life. Which of your spiritual battles is long term? How is your stance in these battles different than in short-term skirmishes?

4. When have you battled the evil within or the evil without for yourself or someone you love? How did the Lord reveal Himself?

The Prayer That Must Be Written
Treasuring Love

One generation commends your works to another;

they tell of your mighty acts.

Ps 145:4

I began to hear about my husband's grandmother not long after Richard and I started dating. Though she had gone on to heaven, her reputation hadn't diminished—not a mite. Her name was Emma Bald Ekhoff, of strong German stock and stronger Christian conviction.

Dietrich "Dick" Ekhoff and Emma, as the story went, had persevered through many hardships from snows so deep their children were afraid Santa wouldn't visit, through the destitution of the Great Depression and World War II. They raised three tall handsome sons in the process: identical twins Ralph (Richard's dad) and Willis were the oldest, and Harold was born several years later.

Richard's boyhood weekends were sometimes spent with his grandparents. His grandfather was a gentle, hearty farmer, and Richard adored him. They palled about the farm together tending the garden and caring for the horses, and cattle, and such. Richard still treasures the handmade sling arrow made for him by that dear man.

Emma tackled the work of country life like a major general. She was known in the community for her baked goods and had plenty of practice perfecting the art as she made all her own bread and kept the cookie jar full of her famous molasses cookies. Emma was a little too no-nonsense and staunchly good to be adored, but she was certainly respected.

The farmhouse walls were adorned with "religious art" as we call it today, pictures of Jesus' earthly ministry. I still have her 8 x 10's of Jesus in a white robe at His ascension, and an unusual black and white print of Jesus surrounded by children of different nationalities. Richard's favorite was a color print of Jesus seated beneath a tree with children on His lap and before Him. He likes to imagine himself there as he prays, even after all these years.

Each evening without fail Emma and Dick retired to the living room for "prayer time," and when he visited, Richard was required to join them. Intercession went on and on—almost an hour—while Dick and Emma prayed aloud for every leader by name and every known need in detail. Poor, spiritually rich, little boy thought it would never end!

He then joined them at their home church, First United Methodist Church (Bixby, Oklahoma) on Sunday mornings. Dick and Emma were pillars in their congregation—especially Emma who had very strong opinions about faith in practice and publicized them freely. She did NOT believe in drinking or card playing. And once when the youth group set up a fundraiser in the fellowship hall she swept in and told them that they were like the moneychangers in the Temple and to remove the display—immediately.

Eventually their pious, industrious days were complete, and Dick and Emma died full of good years, faithful to the end.

In due season Richard and I were married and settled in the Bixby community. The first church we visited was his grandparent's little Methodist church. Halfway through our first Sunday morning in the "meet and greet" segment, the perky choir director (Lucy later became a close friend) slipped out of the choir loft and greeted us enthusiastically. When Richard mentioned our last name, she asked,

"Are you related to the late Emma and Dick?" which of course, we were. At Richard's affirmative, she shared her memories of Emma, in particular her "beautiful prayers."

The Lord called us to join that faith family in the next months, and whenever Richard and I were introduced, we received the gushing testimony about Emma's prayers. Most of the descriptions included how articulate they were and how when she prayed it was as if "the Lord Himself entered the room." The requests lifted by Emma Bald Ekhoff evidently reached the throne room of heaven.

More years passed. The saints who had known Dick and Emma gradually passed away until we seldom heard their names, but I continued grateful for their influence in Richard's life and their heritage in our home church. As I inscribed their names on the "Our Family Tree" page of baby book after baby book, I wondered about the fervent intercession sent up from the quaint living room of the farmhouse and Emma's rich prayers at the Methodist church. Had they prayed for our children or me? Was part of the blessing we enjoyed the result of their faithful petitions? Oh how I wished I had heard even one of those prayers!

One afternoon while going through old boxes we came across some of Emma's kitchen utensils and nick-knacks—and among the rusting remains was her journal. Of course her sons had first dibs, but as soon as I could, I seized it. Opening the small, brown volume, I began to read with expectation! There was an entry for almost every day of the year 1942. I read until the final word, then closed the cover and set it away. Here is the lamentable truth: There was nothing there.

March 2: "Did a big washing. Dick helped me."
March 3: "Did my ironing and darned socks."
March 8: "All went to church. Douglas was here for dinner. Quite windy."
March 9: "Cleaned up the cellar. Beautiful day. Wrote letters."

Interesting? Yes, because these were the details of mid-century farming life. But it was only a bare glimpse of the bare beams. The most passionate sentence in a year of entries was, "Today is Dick's birthday. I love him so."

Consider with me. What if she had recorded her molasses cookie recipe or the name of her favorite book? What do you think it would have meant to me to have the main point of a sermon that she learned to live by, her life verse, or her goal for the year? Might I have been encouraged by several lines about raising boys? How influential would a nugget of practical godly advice, or better yet what she loved about Jesus and why? How momentous would it have been to have had a single written prayer—just *one*? But there was nothing, absolutely nothing.

Emma's little book is before me now, and I have to wonder: Would she have written differently if she had known how much I wanted to know about her relationship with God? Would she have wanted her experience in prayer to be included in my book on prayer? Most certainly she would have.

Now we come to the purpose of this chapter. We are in conversation with the God of the universe and our very personal Lord in the present tense. This conversation is the substance of the prayer that must be written. Seventy years from now when the box of our faded trinkets is opened by a generation we have never met, what greeting will pour forth in the light of the attic window? Is there anything we would like to say about family? About FAITH? Since we have the chance to do better, what should we do with the opportunity?

Prudence

Prudence is the ability to act now in preparation for future events. Noah Webster's 1828 Dictionary[19] states that prudence is being "circumspect; practically wise; careful of the consequences." It is wise to determine now what will be valuable to us later. What then constitutes value? When we look back over the week, year, or our whole lives, I believe it will be how we did our *relationships* that will matter most. And our relationship with the Lord is the most valuable relationship of all. So writing the conversation of our life in prayer is prudent—very prudent. Here are some of the many reasons:

- The history of God's intervention in our lives is cumulative in nature. It reveals God as a manifold Person and teaches us to trust Him.
- The last thing God said is often our instruction for the present crisis or crossroads. We would do well to record what God is revealing so we have the information we need when questions arise or assurances are needed.
- What we journal is the core of our testimony. It's fresh. It's transparent. It's riveting. Our personal experience is a vital witnessing tool.
- The written conversation is a place where our thoughts may be discerned and compared. Retained, they are available for deeper reflection in other seasons.
- The history of our relationship with God provides a framework for our future. In hindsight, people, events, and experiences weave themselves into a pattern, a direction that may position us to move forward in the center of God's will.
- Journaling reveals growth. There comes the joyful day when the record of the conversation substantiates measurable Christian maturity.
- Even if we don't believe we'll need the revelation later, someone else may, and we thereby preserve it as a gift for another. God's investment in our lives is not ours alone. Our written conversation with the Lord is a treasure storehouse of potential insight, especially for our families. It is a spiritual legacy for people we may never meet.

Journaling 101

Part of honoring the Lord is esteeming what He says so much that we feel compelled to hold or retain His communication, i.e., the prayer that must be written. When we think God is speaking, or we have a valuable thought that is directed to Him, we should write it down. When the nugget is safely recorded, we can walk away in peace. The One, who writes His law on our hearts values—even champions—recorded information:

- "Write this on a scroll as something to be remembered . . ." (Ex. 17:14).
- "Write down these words, for in accordance with these words I have made a covenant with you and with Israel" (Ex. 34:27).
- "Now write down this song and teach it to the Israelites" (Deut. 31:19).
- "Go now, write it on a tablet for them, inscribe it on a scroll, that for the days to come it may be an everlasting witness" (Isa. 30:8).

Journaling is one of the best ways to responsibly record and preserve the prayer that must be written. If you are thinking, "No thanks, writing isn't my gift." or if your guilt sensor is going off because you feel that you should journal but hate the very thought of it, or if you've already tried and failed—read on.

Recording your conversation with God doesn't mean you'll be locked into the drudgery of a "to do list." It certainly doesn't mean that you must like to write. Journaled entries do not need to include a great many details or even be arranged in sentences and paragraphs.

There are only three components to an adequate journal entry: a title (to help you find it later), a date (so you can place it within the context of other events), and what you and Jesus say to each other. This can be recorded as a list, outline, statement, question, or quote. The number of words, and the excellence of articulation are inconsequential.

I have found that three fourths of the battle of journaling is won by having a place prepared to receive the conversation. Scattered scraps of paper and church bulletins won't do for this precious practice because the subject matter is too valuable. A journal is a necessity. A handwritten journal should have bound pages (as opposed to spiral bound pages which tend to fall out) and printed lines for neat, readable print. A good electronic journal is stored in an accessible file and backed up regularly.

I have three journals: One journal often travels with me for quick, messy note taking. The second I call "God's Story." It is the consolidated cream of my relationship with my Father. These volumes have become so valuable to me that I try not to take it out of the house anymore. I also have a computer file called "Wisdom" that categorizes online articles and various teachings.

I am a passionate journaler, but not a proponent of journaling for the sake of journaling. It's too much work, and I'm too busy and too tired to invest in meaningless writing. I only journal what the Lord reveals to me, and my reflection or reply back to Him. I do not write every day or even every week. On the other hand, there are days that I can't hurry to my journal fast enough or write long enough to record what God has just said or done. The prayer that must be written is passion driven. Below is my definition of worthy matters, that which constitutes valuable conversation.

Worthy Matters

- Scripture verses that bring revelation and what they reveal
- Questions I'm holding before the Lord or ideas to research, and what He reveals about them.
- The memorials (God met me here)
- Concerns, needs, answers to prayers
- Wisdom nuggets: concise quotes from sermons, books, or songs, etc. that speak in a meaningful way (For longer quotes, I print a copy and affix it to a journal page. I use scrapbook quality, double-stick tape or staple them.)
- Godly advice
- God's direction in times of decision, leaps of faith
- A teaching or sermon outline that I feel God wants me to remember and put into practice
- The movement of God in my life or sphere of influence, or enemy movement for battle strategy
- Lessons learned from experience
- Revelation or hidden truths revealed—"Oh, now I understand!"
- Corrections and repentance
- Foundations and principles
- Commitments and goals
- Discernment, reflection, and meditation
- Dreams, visions, and prophecy
- Miracles

- Examples of character that I want to emulate or avoid: These are impressed on me by the Holy Spirit from the lives of biblical saints, characters in books, historical figures or present-day people. Memorial services are excellent places to hear God speak on this topic.
- Letters or cards that encourage me (Again, I use scrapbook quality, double-stick tape or staple them.)

In short:
- Write what the Lord is revealing.
- Write what you are saying to God.
- Write what brings the Lord rightful credit and glory.
- Write what you should remember.
- Write what could increase the wisdom or faith of those who may read your journal later.

Habits for Gaining Wisdom

A habit that greatly facilitates rich journaling is the ability to recognize wisdom. Wisdom is how God thinks, what God says, and what God does. The idea is to remain curious and alert—even ravenous—as the Lord unfurls His character and ways. This is called spiritual hunger. Becoming sensitive to His presence, voice, and movement takes practice, but with a little discipline it becomes a habit, then an obsession, then the reason we live. There are many habits that facilitate the acquisition of wisdom. Here are some of the best:

- Ask and keep on asking. Ask the Lord for discernment to recognize and assimilate His wisdom (Matt. 7:7, James. 1:5), then expect Him to reveal it. In anticipation, lean forward in the Spirit. Eagerly desire His voice with the attitude of Samuel, "Speak, Lord, for your servant is listening" (1 Sam. 3:10).
- Feed on the written Word as daily bread.
- Be willing to do what it takes to be immersed in the anointing of God. Go to places and sit with people who share godly wisdom. My friend Mary Beth says, "Just show

up." The anointing of the Spirit in those moments cannot be duplicated.

- Cultivate curiosity. Pose questions before God. Let the questions hang suspended until it pleases Him to reveal the answer, or He directs action or study. I also keep a running list of thought-provoking questions—some for personal evaluation and vision, some to ask people I respect that I may tap the wisdom they have gained from their study and experience. The right questions yield astounding answers and wise answers can change the course of our lives.

- Watch for doubles and triples. When the Lord puts the same wisdom in multiple places, He is adding an exclamation mark! I have also found that the Holy Spirit says similar things all over the earth in waves as He directs His Church. Watchmen see His heart and let Him shake their lives.

- Meditate on revealed wisdom to discover its facets of light and life and love. Relish it. Experiment with it. Study to understand.

- Reread your journals to gain the full benefit of what has been stored. Each entry builds and connects the larger story. Wisdom is a cumulative treasure with increasing value. As Solomon states, "[Wisdom] is a tree of life to those who take hold of her" (Prov. 3:18).

The following Proverbs passage describes the pursuit of wisdom. I have italicized the actions that yield the "garland of grace" and the "glorious crown" of wisdom: "*Take hold* of my words with all your heart; *keep* my commands, and you will live. *Get* wisdom, *get* understanding; *do not forget* my words *or turn away* from them. *Do not forsake* wisdom, and she will protect you; *love* her, and she will watch over you. The beginning of wisdom is this: *Get* wisdom. Though it cost all you have, *get* understanding. *Cherish* her, and she will exalt you; *embrace* her, and she will honor you. She will give you a garland to grace your head and present you with a glorious crown" (Prov. 4:4–9, emphasis mine).

Never Too Late

I learned firsthand about the value of our written conversations with God when I began to write chapter one of this book. How thankful I was that my parents had taken the time to write some of the details of their glorious testimony. I felt rich!

During my dad's seminary years, he documented his healing in a six-page paper. After his death, the rough draft and final manuscript with its scribbled grade and a brief note from a seminary professor were packed away and lost. By the time his testimony came into my hands, all that was left were the first three pages of the handwritten rough draft with Dad's scrawled additions squeezed into the margins. Thankfully, before this book received its final edit, a copy of the testimony was discovered in an obscure drawer and returned to us. We received it with grateful tears. (Thanks, Karen!)

A few years after Dad's death, my mom purposed to write her version of their testimony. She handwrote the first half in wondrous detail, beginning with the events of winter 1966 through the spring of 1967 with the hope to publish it. Her sister volunteered to type her notes and began the editing process. But when Mom saw the corrections, she became demoralized by the magnitude of the project and set it aside. She didn't return to the calling to write until age seventy-five. She has just completed her book *The Lamp, Be Aglow and Burning with the Spirit*, which highlights the cream of a lifetime of walking with the Lord. She is proof that it's never too late to begin the prayer that must be written.

Those who know the Lord have a story to remember and a witness to share. No, not everyone is called to write a book! —but each of us can recognize, record, and live the relational wisdom of God. The best time to begin is now, right where we are. Though His thoughts and ways are high above all things, He is revealing Himself to us every day. What wondrous love is this? Love is a Person, and He should be rightfully treasured.

Going Deeper
Questions for Small Group Discussion

1. Do you have written family testimonies from past generations among your earthly treasures? What do they mean to you?

2. If you could ask one person in your family (living or deceased) to speak into your life, who would it be? What would you like for him/her to share with you?

3. What do you want the people you love the most to know about your life? Have you written that information and preserved it? If not, what is the next step in the process?

4. How do you feel about journaling? Share your experience or lack thereof. What steps can you take now to ensure that your conversation with the Lord is valued and recorded? Review the list of "Worthy Matters." Which do you consider valuable enough to remember and write down?

5. Wisdom in its purest form is the character, actions, and words of God. Do you love wisdom? Review the list of habits that facilitate the acquisition of wisdom. Which ones would you like to pursue?

6. Are you called to be a writer? What are you called to write? What is your next step toward realizing that dream?

The Prayer That Must Have Truth
The Perspective of Love

. . . the truth will set you free."
John 8:32

The information in this chapter is based on the writing and teaching of Dr. Edward Smith. It contains my testimony and my personal, simplified version of Dr. Smith's extensive teaching. For more information visit http://www.transformationprayer.org. You will be glad you did!

Richard and I were attending a long-awaited national parenting conference in Tulsa. As part of the leadership team, we were in charge of setting out boxed lunches, manning the prayer room, and assisting guest speakers. Between these responsibilities we attended the sessions.

In the past, rich conferences like these had stockpiled my parenting pantry for months and goodness knows I needed the wisdom—2012 had been a difficult year for the Ekhoff family. But the teaching and fellowship that had so often developed and thrilled me now seemed burdensome, even torturous. Duty was the only thing that kept me in the building.

At one point I had just been seated for a breakout session when I realized I couldn't possibly stay. Anxiety was escalating to such a degree, I felt compelled to rush from the room. Suppressing tears, I was hastily gathering my belongings to make an escape before the speaker reached the podium. As if on cue, the young mother in front of me lifted a fussy infant from his carrier, and I offered to walk him just outside the room. Closing the door quietly behind me was sweet relief.

After ducking and flinching all weekend, we were finally able to pack up, shake hands all around, and go home. The ordeal was over, but I knew that the Lord had uncovered an abscess in my soul.

In the days following the conference, I resolutely made an about face and marched myself back through my memories of meetings and tasks, searching for the places where the most emotional pain was secreted. Along with the near anxiety attack at the breakout session, I remembered meeting a group of eager young parents just leaving lunch when I'd felt the uncharacteristic desire to hide until they had passed. I had resented most of the teaching. I had even sidestepped my closest friends.

By choosing to revisit the pain of these experiences, I was finally able to name the driving emotion. The truth was that I'd been embarrassed, even ashamed to attend the conference, which led to a second question: What was I thinking or believing that made me ashamed to attend a seminar at the center of my ministry calling or face my dearest friends? After some soul searching I was able to articulate a statement that sounded completely true.

I am disqualified.

Just repeating it to myself brought unbidden tears to my eyes. Oh, how it hurt to admit that. All my parenting pain surfaced to mock me. Most days I was doing home things well, but deep down I knew I was not the mother I should be. I wondered if I ever had been. Who was I to attend a conference with really good parents? Who was I to serve in a parenting ministry at all? I was a fake. Believing that I was "disqualified" seemed validated by my concrete personal experience.

I now understood that beneath my super-parent facade, I had worn a badly bruised soul to the conference, and the themes and group dynamics had mercilessly prodded my hidden wounds. It helped to know why I'd felt like running, but this was only half of the journey to my healing. Unless the belief (which was really a lie) was countered by the power of truth, it would surely return in similar circumstances. So holding the belief "I am disqualified" before the Lord—who *is* Truth—I asked for His perspective. "Lord, what is the truth about my parenting? Am I disqualified? What do you want me to know about that?"

He didn't speak in that moment, so I waited expectantly, knowing He would speak when it pleased Him. Over the next weeks I often repeated this prayer, sometimes raising my cupped hand into the air as a symbol of lifting the belief for His dictum. "Lord, *I* say I'm disqualified—what do *You* say?" One morning He spoke, and what He said made all the difference, both then and now.

Healing

Now, I'm a tea person. You know the type. To me, steaming tea in a pretty mug is fortification and ambiance. I start most days with a mugful for good measure. On this midsummer morning, I had a few sprigs of mint from my herb garden in a vase on the counter and fresh lemons in the fridge. For a special treat I tweaked two or three mint leaves from a stem in the vase, crushed the leaves between my fingers and added them to my cup, followed by a spritz of lemon. Then I held my minty, lemony fingers to my nose and drew a deep, deep breath. That fragrance should be bottled and marketed with the title "The First Day of Summer Vacation" —it's that intoxicating. Sipping my tea like ambrosia, I headed to the breakfast table.

Suddenly, I remembered the question I was holding before the Lord. Placing my mug on the table, I earnestly repeated the prayer again. "Lord, I say that I'm disqualified. What do You say?" His answer came with quiet authority, taking me by surprise.

"You are <u>not</u> disqualified. You are *fragrant!*"

You can imagine that the word "fragrant" made an explicit impression as the fragrant tea was still before me.

"I—am—fragrant?"

I stood transfixed wondering what He could mean. Then the Lord gave the interpretation: "Your parenting pressure has bruised you in the same way you bruised the mint leaves and lemon slice, but it has released something lovely—fragrance."

As this truth registered, the old rags of my humiliating belief were surpassed by the splendor of God's perspective. I was shocked—then thankful—then humbled—then awed. Like a virtual Cinderella, I could hardly grasp that I was the same person I'd been the moment before. Immersed in my Father's favor, I could no longer believe I was disqualified. It was impossible to believe anything but the truth He had just revealed. His peace spread out and took up residence.

Then the Lord disclosed a second truth. "It pleased Me to bruise you."

My bruising had pleased Him? What would you have asked in that moment? —that was my question, too. "But why, Father?"

Patiently, He brought me to His perspective. "Dear one, remember the cross. When Jesus was crushed for your transgressions and bruised for your iniquities, His sacrifice pleased Me for His sake and yours. Suffering couldn't disqualify Him; it made Him a fragrant offering" (Isa. 53:5, Eph. 5:2). So my suffering and sacrifices had been a fragrant offering to the Lord! He saw the Ekhoff family struggles as fragrant, sacrificial love for one another, not disqualifying failures.

In the reflective pause that followed, the Lord reminded me of one of my own prayers. Just a few months before, I'd been reading Philippians 3 and had come to this passage: "I want to know Christ—yes, to know the power of his resurrection and participation in his sufferings, becoming like him in his death, and so, somehow, attaining to the resurrection from the dead" (Phil. 3:10–11). At the time I had wondered about this unusual description of fellowship. The *joys* of fellowship I understood, but fellowshipping with Jesus in His *suffering* was foreign to me. Well, if there was a way to know Christ more through His sufferings, then I like Paul wanted the honor of participating. So I asked Him to teach me. I hadn't thought about that request since, but the Lord hadn't forgotten. He never forgets our prayers.

Meditating on these verses over the next weeks brought further revelation. I discovered that this type of fellowship has to do with aligning our hearts with His broken heart for sin, pain, and suffering. What a council I had with the Spirit as I searched the scriptures and scribbled in my journal. Part of the secret of fellowshipping with Jesus through suffering and sacrifice was now mine.

But let me clarify. I'm not advocating enduring physical, emotional or verbal abuse, becoming a self-inflicted martyr, or the pitfalls of co-dependency. I mean the kind of suffering that goes with living the real stuff of the Christian life and becoming fragrant, as Christ is fragrant—*with mercy.* I have seen Jesus in His passion as never before since the moment this truth came to me and the truth has set me free (John 8:32).

Principles of the Prayer That Must Have Truth

This testimony illustrates the healing potential of the prayer that must have truth. It is only one of many such holy conversations with the Lord, my Healer that has released me to live in the freedom of His perspective. The Lord initiated the conversation by revealing that I was bound by a belief (lie) that hadn't originated from His love for me. He allowed the conference and my painful emotions to alert me to my need for His wisdom. My response was to present my exposed emotions and statement of belief back to Him for His perspective. Truth dispelled deception and changed the atmosphere of my soul.

The prayer that must have truth isn't a formula, but there are steps that may facilitate the pursuit of God's truth, bringing transformational emotional healing:

- Harnessing triggers for what they reveal
- Identifying painful emotions
- Uncovering the hidden belief (lie)
- And finally holding the belief before the Lord of Truth

Harnessing Triggers

A trigger is a recent situation that has invoked more emotion than was warranted; in other words, the emotion doesn't seem proportional to the event. No one is exempt from hidden beliefs that are based in lies. We all have them whether we are conscious of them or not. At some point a situation will trigger our beliefs, and our painful emotions will manifest. The first step toward emotional healing is to harness triggers for what they reveal.

In my conference experience, my disproportionate emotions were the clue that I was experiencing a trigger—my mind and my emotions were definitely not in agreement. It would've been easy to blame-cast my anxiety on my husband, my friends, the stress of serving, or the content of the conference, but they were not the cause of my pain. The pain was caused by my hidden belief.

Triggers are a like a test. In the same way that exams reveal the information students have stored in their minds, triggers reveal the beliefs we have stored in our hearts.

—To harness a trigger ask: Were my emotions disproportionate to the event? Am I willing to own my reaction? Am I willing to harness my overt emotions for what they reveal about my hidden beliefs?

Identifying the Emotion

After the parenting conference, I had to decide if I would put the whole experience behind me or revisit those torturous emotions. In the end I was willing to face the frustration and sting to have the truth and healing. When we let our emotions have a voice—even if they say irrational or unchristian things—they can reveal the belief system that drives them. The presenting pain, fear, or anger (anger is the protective covering for underlying pain and fear) often point to an underlying core emotion—in my case, the emotion was shame.

It is helpful to avoid "preaching" to negative emotions when they surface, hoping they'll behave and stand down. Suppressing them protects the belief (the lie) and postpones the healing. The same emotional pain will only resurface at the next trigger. It is such a relief to confess our raw emotion to the One who cares.

—To uncover and name painful emotions ask: How did the incident make me feel? Be specific. When several emotions are present, select the most painful one or the one that embodies the others.

Uncovering the Belief (Lie)

Identifying the painful emotions I'd experienced at the conference helped me uncover the lie I believed, "I am disqualified." As life happens, we naturally internalize beliefs about events, people, God, and ourselves. Some are beneficial, others benign. Still others are deceptive, even toxic. For better or for worse our beliefs color our perceptions and fuel our reactions.

Satan uses these deceptions to pit us against our Father. His voice breeds shame, discord, and death. In contrast, the Lord speaks honor, peace, and life. By examining the fruit of our beliefs, we can name the author of them.

Simply naming a belief (lie) can be freeing in itself. Snatched from the shadows and shaken out for examination, the painful statement begins to release its grip and become vulnerable to change. But an invasive lie does not voluntarily leave. Only Jesus can bring revelatory truth to bear; He is our Wonderful Counselor and Prince of Peace (Isa. 9:6).

—To discover the lie that is driving emotional pain ask: What do I believe about myself, others or God? What am I repeating to myself under the surface of everyday life? When did I first begin to think this way? Based on those past experiences, who do I say I am?

—Sometimes finishing an "I am" statement can help articulate the belief. In the light of the emotions I am experiencing now and similar emotional pain from my past, I admit that I am _____.

Trusting the Lord of Truth

God is perpetually in all times and places. He was and is still in the past, just as He is even now in the present and the future. That means that God is ever present in our personal past and loves us there. His fresh perspective has the power to shatter deception and lies. Jesus said, "The thief comes only to steal and kill and destroy; I have come that they may have life, and have it to the full" (John 10:10). And again, "I am the way and the truth and the life" (John 14:6).

I testify to the Lord's goodness through experience. His word to me was specifically timed, so I could more fully grasp it. The revelation was so potent that it surged through my surface-self to the bleeding places underneath. The Lord's truth interrupted the reigning lie, then purged it. As the revelation registered, the Spirit's peace spread out. Each part of this adventure in prayer brought God's goodness to bear. "What then shall we say in response to all these things? If God is for us who can be against us" (Rom. 8:31)? Oh, friend—know that what He did for me, He is able and willing to do for you.

—To lift a painful belief before the Lord for His truth ask: Lord, what do You want me to know? I generally word my question like this: "Lord, what is the truth? I say _____ (placing my belief in the blank—what do You say?" or "What do You want me to know about _____?"

—Being afraid for the Lord to speak is a trigger in itself. When the lie we believe is against the character of God ask: Do I trust God to speak? What would happen if He spoke? Am I willing to allow God to defend His character? Am I willing to elevate the Lord's opinion above my own?" I often ask, "Lord, what do You want me to know about Your character?"

Peace and Freedom

The revelation of truth is a process. Over a period of years the Lord has healed some of my painful emotions, but I don't walk in full freedom from every lie I believe; I'm not sure that's possible on earth. In the meantime it comforts me to know that Jesus will have the final word over my life, and every lie will eventually bow to Him: "I know Whom I have believed, and am convinced that He is able to guard what I have entrusted to Him until that day" (2 Tim. 1:12b).

The Father wants us to be free from deceptions that enslave us. Beneath the pain, fear, and anger of our lives, there is a deep-seated need and capacity for His powerful truth. The prayer that must have truth is the conversation that gives God permission to supersede our tainted beliefs. The perspective of Love has the power to set us free, and Love is a Person. Halleluiah!

Going Deeper
Questions for Small Group Discussion

1. When have you fellowshipped with Jesus in His suffering (sacrificing for love's sake)?

2. Have you ever experienced a trigger? What emotions did the trigger uncover? When have you experienced similar emotions? (These emotions could be linked to childhood.) What did you believe about yourself in your earliest experience with these emotions? Ask the Lord to help you discern and state your belief: In the light of this experience, I admit that I am _____.

3. Do you want God's perspective about this belief (lie)? Holding it before the Lord ask, "Lord, what do you want me to know about this belief? What is Your perspective? What is the truth?

The Prayer That Must Let Go
Surrendering to Love

Offer the sacrifices of the righteous and trust in the Lord.
Psalm 4:5

My sincere thanks to my dear friends Linda, Charlie and Erin White, who lived this story with such integrity and allowed it to showcase the prayer that must let go. And my gratitude to John Venturella for allowing me to share his song and interview.

In the days before sonograms the girl/boy question remained the Lord's secret until the actual birth of the baby. So it was a real surprise for the White family when the attending gynecologist enthusiastically announced, "Well, you got a girl this time!"

Double-footling breach, dark-headed and dainty, Erin Elizabeth entered the world on June 6, 1974. She completed the family of five at the "White House" with older brothers James, age six, and Bryan, age four, preceding her. Her parents Linda and Charlie were delighted. It was so sweet to think that in addition to the boys, there would be a daughter to share their lives—as only a daughter can.

Pink and frilly baby things were new to Charlie, but not long after Erin's birth he dressed her for an outing all by himself. When

Linda lifted her from the carrier a little later, Erin was modeling the pink panty, ruffle-side front. How was a daddy to know?

With blond curls (her hair grew out blond) and big brown eyes, Erin was an endearing toddler. She faithfully tended her baby dolls—all the while keeping an eye on her brothers, lest she miss one of their escapades. She learned early on how to keep a foothold in the action. When one of them shouted, "Me first!" she countered, "Me second!" and always got to be second.

Wholesome family days blended into years, and Erin grew up. She developed her dad's common sense, her mother's listening ear, her brother James's book smarts, and her brother Bryan's fun-loving nature. Her parents modeled their relationship with the Lord and prayed her through the bumpy mid-teens, what Erin called her "rebellious" time, while her youth pastor taught her to seek God for herself. Thank goodness for teachers who require journaling. Erin's dutiful entries, recorded in snippets over her junior and senior high years, are a penned self-portrait:

> As a child I was always shy, yet curious and willing to learn. I was easily persuaded. I would try anything my brothers suggested. I'm still curious, but I also have my own strong beliefs.
>
> If I meet someone new, the first thing they notice is that I am shy. But when they get to know me, I talk constantly and do things that should embarrass me. I'll try almost anything. I don't take things too seriously or worry on one thing too long. I like to have fun—even if I am by myself. I usually have a smile on my face. People know me as a person who doesn't get mad.
>
> One more thing people notice about me is I like the natural look, and I enjoy "scumming out." I rarely wear a dress, but when I do, people always say, "Oh, Erin looks dressed up today."
>
> The thing I like best about myself is the way that I'm able to talk to people and try to help them out. I am friendly and trustworthy. My friends all know that if there is something wrong, they can come to me; I can't turn people away if they come to me with a problem. If I am unable to help with advice, I'll try to help by getting someone else. I tell people the honest truth even if they don't like the sound of it.
>
> I am very goal-oriented. I like to learn, and I set goals for myself and achieve them. My short-term goals include things as easy as graduating from high school (class of '92) and getting A's. After graduation, I will get my bachelor's degree in

mechanical engineering at Tulsa University. My main goal is to be happy and never afraid to try something new.

As I prepared to write Erin's story, her mother found a spiral bound notebook decorated for a high school class. Erin had artistically arranged magazine cutouts across the cover. Three phrases seemed prophetic: "Where Dreams and Reality Collide," "Make an Impression No One Will Forget" and "Built to Win."

Where Dreams and Reality Collide

In the fall of 1992, Erin entered Tulsa University's engineering program and moved to campus as planned. She charged into the experience with her usual fervor, challenged by the academics and involved in student activities. To her surprise she was elected president of her dorm her sophomore year. In the meantime she met and fell in love with Joey. They became engaged on her twenty-first birthday.

But early winter 1995, the unthinkable interrupted Erin's dreams. The first indication of concern was rapid weight loss—twenty pounds during the month of December alone. Erin's five-foot, four-inch frame was emaciated. Early tests run for a possible thyroid disorder came back negative.

James—now married and in medical residency in Kansas City, and Bryan—transitioning to Colorado for a new job, were both home for a merry family Christmas. It was good just to be together.

In January an exasperated Erin was slated for a hospital stay and extensive scans. She had no time for testing with a short five days until classes opened (her last semester at TU), but there was no other option, and she finally submitted. Her parents thought perhaps she was suffering from Irritable Bowel Syndrome or worst-case Crohn's Disease. The scans revealed a sizable malignant tumor in her large intestine.

Erin's initial concern was diminished as her father had been diagnosed with colon cancer and after surgery was cancer free. She optimistically reasoned that her outcome would be like his, a complete recovery. Understandably, her parents were grief stricken. I can never forget the anguish on her father's face in those days.

Between January and April Erin underwent a round of radiation to shrink the tumor in preparation for surgery, which was performed on Good Friday of Easter weekend. Immediately after surgery Linda and Charlie were summoned to a private post-op consultation with the surgeons. The cancer had spread well beyond the intestinal wall into the surrounding tissue and liver. Her surgeons had discussed every viable option in the process of surgery. Removing the tumor and a pelvic sweep were deemed too invasive and would have diminished Erin's quality of life. With the addition of a colostomy, the surgeons had closed the incision with the tumor still in place. The next step would be chemotherapy followed in later months by radiation on isolated spots on her bones.

Some families become private in their hour of crisis, but the White family became large and transparent. Our church family tried to serve—and they let us. When hearts are broken, it's a privilege to want to help and be welcomed in to do so. We loved the Whites for that.

Our first response was food. Linda says she didn't cook a single meal—breakfast, lunch or dinner—for seven weeks straight at this point. Our pastor recorded a "soaking" tape and received Erin's calls in the wee hours when she was anxious or in pain. Our youth pastor created a trifold pamphlet with scripture and devotionals. The worship choruses she taught Erin became a major source of faith.

But our best gift was prayer. We were all aware of Erin's immediate daily needs and faithfully prayed over them. As Erin received the answers to our specific prayers, we were strengthened to believe again and again on her behalf. We all experienced the updraft of God's powerful sustenance. He cared so much.

Not long after Erin's surgery, Linda was alone in the car. As hope and fear churned together, a prayer poured forth unbidden and seared tears: "I don't want to let her go, Lord, but if one person could be saved through this, I *release* her." Even as the prayer left her lips, she wanted to grab it back. No, no! That was not what she wanted to say at all. How could she ever let Erin go? But she knew that the Holy Spirit had authored that prayer and she let it stand.

This was Linda's moment to let go. It was the next step in her established love relationship with her Father, and a most loving act on behalf of her daughter.

Erin had become characterized by prefacing potentially painful thoughts about her outcome with, "Mom, I don't want this to upset you, but when I die . . ."

So Linda was free to be just as honest. "Erin, I don't want this to upset you, but this was my prayer . . . " and Erin received the confession graciously.

Releasing Erin to be an adult was the next faith hurdle for her parents. When she expressed her frustration with her medical team for addressing their comments exclusively to her parents, Linda and Charlie stepped back from the position of decision makers and empowered her to determine her own treatment. She also wanted to continue living in her apartment at TU, even though the last two required classes for her degree would not be offered again until January. This sacrifice was painful. They wanted her at home, so they could enjoy and protect her. But in this too their wills were finally relinquished to Jesus.

Make an Impression No One Will Forget

Cancer has a way of purifying the best and pruning the rest. For Erin the unimportant fell away, and the important became priceless. "I love you" slipped into her conversations and actions. She surprised the Ekhoff children with a balloon bouquet, started a Bible study in her dorm, and shared her testimony with the church youth group. This is not to say she was impervious to the realities of cancer. She still had her personal frustrations, painful nights, and private tears, but she didn't allow these to limit her.

In May 1996 Erin met with family friend John Venturella who was composing the music for an upcoming CD release. He asked if he could interview her and write a song in her honor. Erin made an unforgettable impression on John, and with her permission he released the interview to the *Tulsa World* where her testimony blessed many more. Here is Erin's perspective of life with cancer from his article:

> This experience has been a major part of my life; it has changed the way I think and behave. And even in the worst-

case scenario, should I die from this cancer, it will still be a very powerful experience in the lives of my family and friends. I don't know which outcome would have a bigger impact on other people's lives.

I don't want to die so early in my life, but I realize that I'm no longer afraid of it. I also believe it has to do with God's timing, not mine. I formerly had my own schedule for my life— when I would graduate, get married, etc. However, it is now evident that was not meant to be, and I have taken this as a learning experience and put my faith in God's plan. Statements from my life application Bible say something to the effect that God did not put us on this earth to make us happy. This has meant a lot to me in regards to understanding my purpose.

If I could speak into the lives of others dealing with cancer, first, I would share that their cancer is not something that they created in their body or that they can fix. I would encourage them not to be afraid. What I mean is that you can be afraid, but you don't let fear ruin or rule your life. Let God show you what to do with your life. He will lead you. Don't worry, just do what you can today: be aware, be a witness, be a servant. The worship chorus "You are My Hiding Place" reminds me that when I go to Jesus, I can be a child and not have to appear strong. I can be afraid and weak, and it's okay. With His help I can get through anything that comes.

Today's heroes have struggles and hardships in their lives. It is important that we take our life experiences and use them for the good no matter how bad they are. I am hopeful that I am being a great example for people that look up to me. I believe now that I was born to make a difference in this world, to affect people.

My guiding Bible verse is a paraphrase of Romans 8:28 given to me by a family friend who has had cancer. "The Lord may not definitely have planned that this should overtake me, but He most certainly has permitted it. Therefore though it were an attack of the enemy, by the time it reaches me, it has the Lord's permission and all is well. He will make it work together with all of life's experiences for good."

After the interview, John Venturella composed and published "Erin's Song."

Erin's Song[20]

There was a time my life was simple and well-planned
I built my hopes, my dreams on earthly sand
Then came the day the floods washed my dreams away

I said goodbye to the child I was that day

Chorus
Though my life's been turned around, now I stand on solid ground
In God's arms I rest through each earthly test,
Though my life's been turned around, now I stand on solid ground
In God's arms I rest, in God's care.

Lord, help me be a willing servant to Your call,
And by Your grace to share Your love with all,
To touch a life and make a difference on my way
Thy will be done through my life each day.
Ending
In God's care, in my Father's arms
Embraced by grace, in God's care

Built to Win

Erin had cancer, yes, but that didn't cancel her personal goals. In January 1997, she eagerly enrolled in her final two classes at TU. But now Erin's strength began to give way. By April 11 chemo treatments were discontinued, and she moved home. With tenacity and her mother's help, she managed classes through Wednesday, April 16.

On Friday night, April 18, the president of Tulsa University and some of Erin's professors presented her engineering diploma in her family room. Erin couldn't quite believe it was hers, but they insisted that she had more than earned it. The rapid growth of tumors had so changed Erin's appearance since they had last seen her—a single week for some of them—that her professors openly wept as they said their goodbyes to Charlie on the front porch. Their unmasked grief startled him. He suddenly realized that His little girl's life was ending. This was Charlie's moment to let go.

The next morning Erin was able to visit a bit from bed, but by Saturday night, she was slipping into a coma and becoming restless. As Linda ministered in the quiet room, Erin began to whisper. "I can't do this any more. God, I just can't do this any more." Waking Charlie, they slipped into her bed, one on each side. "You have your diploma. You have seen your brothers. We'll be okay. You don't have to fight any more. We love you." In these moments Erin released her own life to God for the final time, and a peace that could be felt enveloped the room.

On Sunday afternoon as her brother and sister-in-law James and Jan lingered at her bedside, Erin suddenly opened her eyes and said, "I'm halfway there, and this room is filled with people." These were her last words on earth. Erin slipped into Heaven not many hours later. She had fought the good fight—and won.

Understanding the Prayer That Must Let Go

Also called "the prayer of relinquishment" (Katherine Marshall, *Beyond Ourselves*[21]), "the death of a dream" (Bill Gothard, *Institute for Basic Youth Conflicts*[22]), and "the prayer that never fails" (Jan Karon, *At Home in Mitford*[23]), the prayer that must let go is the altar of the soul. An altar is the specific time and place where we release or submit our will to God and leave the outcome in His control. In these moments we lay the dearest parts of who we are and those we love before God and step back, not knowing what will happen next. This solitary, suspended moment can feel perilously risky.

Where Wills Clash

There are three distinct forces at work at our altars: our will, our enemy's will, and our Father's will. Our will is what we want. It is the strong force behind making what we think best a reality. Unfortunately, our will is limited by our finite understanding. It is characterized by desiring the way of least pain. It is sometimes biased with selfishness.

The will of the enemy is to kill, steal, and destroy (John 10:10). As the father of lies, satan's deceptions exclusively yield evil (John 8:44). His motive is to destroy our relationship with our Father by defaming His Name.

The incorruptible will of the Father is perfectly good and blessed. He only desires those things that reflect His own character: whatever is true, noble, right, pure, lovely, admirable, excellent, or praiseworthy (Phil. 4:8). God never merges His will with another. To do so would contaminate Wisdom. His heart leans toward us, and our prayers move Him, but we cannot dictate His will.

Submitting our will to God simultaneously overturns our shortsighted bias and satan's diabolical schemes. Here is a sure truth. God can redeem any will that is submitted to Him. Even satan's will presented to God by His people is redeemed for our benefit through the cross. That which is submitted becomes consecrated, set apart for holy purposes. To those who are the called according to His purpose (in other words, those who have submitted their wills to His purposes) all things work together for good (Rom. 8:28).

In their crisis with cancer, Linda, Charlie and Erin willed what was pleasant and expected—a happy, normal life. Who wouldn't? Satan willed to destroy Erin's physical and spiritual life and discredit the reputation of God. But God, our God, willed to redeem the enemy's plan and profoundly bless the Whites. He willed to bring glory to Himself through exploits on their behalf. And as the White family relinquished their wills to His higher purposes, that is exactly what He did.

Let's consider again Erin's working paraphrase of Romans 8:28: "The Lord may not definitely have planned that this should overtake me, but He most certainly has permitted it. Therefore, though it were an attack of the enemy, by the time it reaches me, it has the Lord's permission, and all is well. He will make it work together with all of life's experiences for good." This idea was too big for me when Erin first quoted it and lived it before me. It made me angry to think that cancer had come to her. Cancer can never be the will of God. But Erin didn't say that the cancer was God's will; she was living on the redeemed side of what the enemy meant for evil, trusting that God was redeeming it all and working His goodness into her life—and He was. "*Submit* yourselves, then, to God. Resist the devil, and he will flee from you" (James. 4:7, emphasis mine).

As you have read Erin's story, perhaps you have been inspired to risk more in prayer, but can't imagine submitting your will in similar ways. What happens if you see the value of the prayer that must let go, but are not willing to pray it? The next best prayer is "Lord, I am willing to be made willing." This prayer releases His strength to begin to make the transaction possible. "[Not in your own strength] for it is God Who is all the while effectually at work in you [energizing and creating in you the power and desire], both to will and to work for His good pleasure and satisfaction and delight" (Phil. 2:13, AMPC).

The prayer that must let go is relational prayer centered in a love relationship with Jesus. Because He knows that the relinquishment of our will can be filled with pain—He knows this from personal experience (see John 3:16, Luke 22:42), He sustains us in the midst of it. In the act of release, the Spirit bestows a surge of grace, and His presence becomes the benediction. Praise His name! As we let go, we free fall into the arms of Love. His glories follow.

Glory

The prayer that must let go is sacrificial in nature, but it is also a conduit of glory. I do not mean to say that the full victory is immediately seen, but it does mean that it is immanent. Like Jesus, who "for the joy set before him, he endured the cross, scorning its shame" (Heb. 12:2), we can set our eyes on the joy set before us. Here are four compelling glories of relinquishment for meditation as we risk the prayer that must let go.

Epic Heroes

Pause with me and call to mind the biblical, historical, and present day heroes that most impact our lives. One of the notable commonalities of those we admire is their altar experience. In this moment their predetermined will skids to a halt against God's higher purpose for their lives, and they choose to submit themselves—even if it means sacrifice or suffering. Inevitably, the agony of their relinquishment is their finest hour, and the events that follow bring lasting influence. In the same way, when we yield our preconceived will and take up the will and call of God, we join the great epic story, a Kingdom adventure that will take us beyond ourselves.

All of us are candidates for hero status. Dwight L. Moody blazoned this statement with his life example: "The world has yet to see what God can do with a man fully consecrated to him. By God's help, I aim to be that man." This is the pledge of those who forsake their own will and devote themselves exclusively to God's purposes in the prayer that must let go.

Wounded Healers

Another conduit of glory is the powerful ministry of wounded healers. When do we genuinely praise God for the pain of relinquishment? For me that moment comes when I bless someone else with the comfort and wisdom I gained at my altar. "Praise be to the God and Father of our Lord Jesus Christ, the Father of compassion and the God of all comfort, who comforts us in all our troubles, so that we can comfort those in any trouble with the comfort we ourselves receive from God" (2 Cor. 1:3–4).

John Venturella shared this thought with Erin during the interview mentioned above: "Sometimes God allows things to occur in our lives, and through these experiences we become sensitized to the needs of others . . . I am convinced that the most effective healers are those who have lived through life-shattering experiences, which then gives them the opportunity to be reborn into a wounded healer." Those who have passed through the fire are positioned to reach back to others as they face altars of their own.

Memorial Stones

Hannah Hurnard has written an allegory called *Hinds' Feet on High Places* that is worth a read. Some describe it as the female counterpart of the classic *Pilgrim's Progress,* and I agree.

The main character is Much-Afraid, a cripple from the village of Much-Trembling. When the Shepherd (Jesus) invites her to the High Places (the seat of His Kingdom) and gives her two formidable guides, Sorrow and Suffering, she embarks on an adventure that will transform her.

The path of the three companions winds through the desert and into the mountains where Much-Afraid must submit her will to the Shepherd again and again. At each altar she chooses an ordinary pebble to remind herself of the lesson learned there and places it in the small brown pouch worn around her neck.

At one point in the treacherous journey, Much-Afraid is tempted to toss her memorial stones away. Removing the pouch and pouring its contents into her lap, she repeats the lesson learned at each altar. After a time of reflection, she concedes, "Though everything in the world should tell me that they are worthless—I cannot part with them." Then she reverently returns the stones to their pouch and sets out with tremulous faith. I will not spoil the ending but to say that the pebbles are not what they seem. Each becomes a gemstone that the Shepherd sets into a crown for her head.

When we are tempted to shun the prayer that must let go, we would be wise to remember the Lord greatly values the relinquishment of our will, and the seemingly ordinary stones of our memorials are priceless.

Soaring Eagles

Finally, when we release our will to God, we receive the glorious updraft of the Spirit's power to live in the midst of pressure and pain without being pinned by it. John Venturella testifies, "When I opened my front door on the day Erin and I met for the interview, I was struck by her fragile condition. She reminded me of a petite sparrow standing in the doorframe. Many times during our discussion as she shared her deep faith in the Lord, the tiny sparrow that I saw initially, became a strong and powerful eagle right before my eyes."

The prayer that must let go releases us and those we love to flight. This is a divine mystery: Stinging injury can become profound healing; trembling weakness can become supernatural strength; grievous loss can become heady increase; rending isolation can become friendship with God. History verifies that the more difficult the release, the more glorious the victory.

In truth every person who witnessed Erin's struggle with cancer was swept up in God's goodness. Linda now testifies that she felt closer to Jesus than at any other time in her life—before or since. Charlie and Linda are now wounded healers with a powerful compassion ministry and are more beloved than anyone I know. Our church family was unified on Erin's behalf in ways that have lasted. And even though we miss her so much, Erin is completely safe and healed in Heaven—rejoicing. In the meantime God is still using her testimony to influence others.

Not long after Erin's death, I felt led to share a prophecy about the next years. The Holy Spirit promised wave upon wave of blessing as reports of the impact of Erin's life surged back to wash Linda and Charlie's feet, and in the moment that they thought that her influence had ended, a fresh wave would surprise them. Just as the Lord promised, His blessings keep flowing right up to this very moment—for as you have read this chapter *you* are being impacted by Erin's testimony. Your response to the prayer that must let go is the next splashing wave upon their shore and yours.

Each of us will face altars of the soul. As we face the risk, let's take comfort in this truth: We are surrendering to Love, and Love is a Person. Blessed assurance!

> *You will go out in joy and be led forth in peace;*
> *the mountains and hills will burst into song before you,*
> *and all the trees of the field will clap their hands.*
> *Instead of the thornbush will grow the juniper,*
> *and instead of briers the myrtle will grow.*
> *This will be for the Lord's renown,*
> *for an everlasting sign, that will endure forever."*
> Isa. 55:12–13

A Letter and Prayer from Linda

Dear friend,

In the days after Erin's death, I had many "whys," "if onlys," and "what ifs." Did Erin know how much she was loved? Did I get to tell her everything that was on my heart? The Lord reassured me that Erin surely knew by the way she had been raised. Even after twenty years of life without Erin, there are still questions like these that have to be held before the Lord and released.

Relinquishing Erin is a process that has continued. The week after Erin died her best friend was married. We attended Amy's ceremony to rejoice with her, but it was a bittersweet time as we realized that we would never be able to help our daughter plan her own wedding. We had to let go of that dream. Also when Erin's friends have babies, we are reminded of the life Erin could have known. We grieve that we will never be able to hold our daughter's children, and once again, we release the dream to the Lord.

I remember reading a devotional in Oswald Chambers' *My Utmost for His Highest* (entry titled "Missionary Munitions," September 10), which said you can't expect to be prepared in the crisis if you are not developing your relationship with the Lord now. It is the preparation you make *before* the crisis that is solid ground when the unexpected hits. The way to come through with the victory is to be pressed into the Lord, be in His Word, and be grounded in prayer. We are so thankful that Erin was grounded in her faith and glorified God as she walked this journey with cancer.

Even though Erin's sixteen-month battle with cancer was one of the worst times in our lives, our family also remembers it as one of the best times in our lives. We've never felt closer to the Lord. We were reminded daily of His provision and what is really important in life.

You don't know until you face something how strong you are. When an unsaved co-worker told me she wished she were strong like me, I told her it wasn't me, but God in me. All the prayers that were being lifted up for our family were answered. Our faithful God knows what is ahead of us today, and He has already prepared His mercy for the path ahead.

May the Lord be your strength!
Love, Linda

Going Deeper
Questions for Small Group Discussion

1. Which parts of Erin's story challenged you the most? Which parts encouraged you to follow her example?

2. Who and what do you love the most? Has the Lord required that any of these treasures be released to Him? How did you respond?

3. What is your will for your life? What is satan's will? What is God's will? Have you submitted your will and satan's will to the pure wisdom and kindness of God's will?

4. Jesus let the joy set before Him strengthen Him as He submitted His will to His Father. Which of the glories of the prayer that must let go visions you most? Why?

The Prayer That Must Worship
Perceiving Love

Not to us, Lord, not to us,
but to your name be the glory,
because of your love and faithfulness.
Ps. 115:1

What shall I return to the Lord
for all his goodness to me?"
Ps. 116:12

The high-profile atheist Bertrand Russell was once asked, "Lord Russell, what will you say when you die and are brought face to face with your Maker?" Russell replied without hesitation: "I shall say, 'God, why did you make the evidence for your existence so insufficient?'" This chapter is my rebuttal. Since the Lord is intentionally and profusely communicating, I think a better question would be—why do we take such pains to ignore Him?

The prayer that must worship is recognizing and responding to God's manifold revelation of Himself. Below are a few treasured memories in this avenue of prayer. Like an accordion photo sleeve filled with faded pictures of beloved children, I smile over them from time to time. Each "snapshot" uniquely invites me to worship—even today.

The Spirit of Jesus began to teach me about worship not long after my introduction to Him in the "Upper Room." I must have been fourteen or so. I was swinging on the tree swing in my grandmother Easley's front yard. I was gazing past a sagging barbed wire fence toward the sunset's reflection on the placid pond beyond, when the Holy Spirit engaged me with fellowship. I felt He was revealing His obvious beauty by delighting me with the quaint scene before me. In these moments I gazed "upon the beauty of the Lord" (Ps. 27:4). Since that time, I often worship Him as the Beautiful One.

Then there was the fine fall morning I traveled with the family of a school chum for a day along the Blue Ridge Parkway of Virginia. We spent the first part of the day at the orchard of a family friend. Bushel baskets of red and green delicious apples had been picked and hauled by wagon that very morning, and we had the delightful task of choosing which variety to taste. Selecting a green delicious, I bit into a foretaste of heaven's fruit. Then I ate a red one. My soul was in the throws of rhapsody! I think it had to do with the autumn tang, the complementary colors of red against green, and the mountain vista. I received this experience as a gift from the Lord because it was. "Taste and see that the Lord is good" (Ps. 34:8). He often reveals Himself as irresistibly wonderful, and I worship Him.

The bravura of sky wonders is another gift and invitation to worship. I once heard Beth Moore describe a trip into the wilds of Africa where the Lord so delighted her with the splendor of the heavens that she stood outside her tent and applauded. When I heard her testimony, I thought, "Why didn't I think of that?" and took up the habit. Deserving of ovation are the moon in its phases, especially at its rising, and the morning star just before dawn on a winter morning. But the constellation Orion is my uncontested favorite. I search for it in the night sky, then let it point me to its Designer. "The heavens declare the glory of God; the skies proclaim the work of his hands" (Ps. 19:1). Jesus reveals Himself as Master Creator and I worship Him.

Beyond nature I love worship experiences with language translations and the multi-colors of culture. One conference worship service of this kind transfigured Jesus before me. It featured the presentation of majestic banners proclaiming specific names of the Lord. There were rich reds with iridescent satin trains, blues and purples accented with silver tassels, and shining gold with fluttering fringe. His glorious name displayed thus in a diverse audience gave me a glimpse of that day soon to come when "every knee should bow. . . and every tongue acknowledge that Christ is Lord, to the praise of God the Father" (Phil. 2:10–11). I saw Jesus "high and lifted up," and it brought my soul to its knees. "Ascribe to the Lord the glory due his name; worship the Lord in the splendor of his holiness" (Ps. 29:2). Jesus revealed Himself as the Name above all names. The announcement of His Name still ushers me into worship.

But my favorite opportunity for worship is teaching with its sweet surprises and rewards. Those of you who have the honor will relate. I am losing myself in the teaching of a point—all but preaching—when suddenly a spark leaps from me to a child in the room. What I just said has landed as a seed in fertile soil. The transaction happens in the privacy of a child's soul then registers in her eyes as a flash of understanding and appreciation. It reminds me of a candle being lit. This too is an invitation to worship. "Wisdom will enter your heart, and knowledge will be pleasant to your soul" (Prov. 2:10). Jesus reveals Himself as the birthplace of Wisdom, and I worship Him.

Strong artistic visuals and awakening wisdom inspire me to worship. But each of us is different. You may be deeply touched by the wheels and sparks of mechanics, the intricacies and exploration of science, the satisfying practicality and orderliness of Math or Computer Science, the creative combinations of landscaping or cooking, the prudence and risk of finance, the simple depth and exultation of music, or the innovative influence of media. The possibilities are endless. But no matter what our personality or interests, the Holy Spirit has the ability to take our breath away as He reveals Jesus in fresh, inspiring ways. These revelations are our personal invitation to worship Him.

Revelation

Many years ago I read *Worship as Jesus Taught It*, by Judson Cornwall.[24] I was impacted by Cornwall's teaching and have been testing his worship theories for myself. This teaching is based on my personal application of his principles of worship. I highly recommend the book for a deeper understanding of worship that I will only skim here.

There are many definitions for worship, but for the purpose of this book, worship is simply recognizing and responding to God's revelation. Revelation is a sudden or dawning insight into the character and ways of God through scripture, prayer, nature, or experience. By revelation I mean fresh understanding built upon the biblical wisdom already at work in our lives. Our response? We *must worship*! It is fitting and right that we should do so, our reasonable service (Rom. 12:1).

Our Father wants us to know Him more and more. Pause, and think reverently of that. He has many things to say to us, more than we can internalize in one sitting, so He slathers His revelation over the days and years of our lives. As the Lord intentionally moves in and around us, the resplendence of His character sparkles like the facets of a diamond in sunlight. When light is refracted in the natural, we see the visible spectrum—a rainbow. In the same way, as the light of our Father's character refracts in our circumstances, we experience love in vivid array. He shows us "great and mighty things which we do not know" (Jer. 33:3). Not all of His revelation is joyous—what breaks His heart will wreck us—but His revelation is always good.

And this is only the beginning of the beginning. The day will come when we see in a "glass dimly" no more. We will see Him as He is (1 Cor. 1:12). What fathomless depth then! But for now a preview of Heaven is ours in the prayer that must worship. For those who are longing to worship the Lord in the routine and extraordinary events of life, here are some principles for recognizing and responding to His revelation.

Revelation and Attentiveness

In earth to Heaven interaction, the Holy Spirit outlines our responsibility with verbs: "search with all your heart," "remain awake," "see and hear," "knock and keep on knocking," "long for," "eagerly desire," "expectantly wait." So we must exercise attentiveness to perceive God's revelation.

Judson Cornwall illustrates the importance of spiritual attention in this way. God was speaking in the days of Jesus' birth. Those who were watching perceived His revelation and worshipped Him—those who were not, missed their visitation. Many looked into the night sky in that season, but only a very few followed the star and worshipped Jesus for who He was. And again, there were many in the temple court when Jesus was presented on His eighth day, but only Simeon and Anna recognized Him as the Lord's Christ and received the honor of worshipping Him.

That's not to say that God must wait for us to pay attention to communicate. Even when we are oblivious, God can and still does reveal Himself. Remember with me: Moses at the burning bush, Mary before the angel Gabriel, and Paul on the road to Damascus—the scriptures are filled with examples. None of these people were in deep prayer or study when God broke into their everyday. When the Lord was ready to reveal Himself—He did. But the daily acquisition of revelation can be a "sit up and pay attention" activity.

Revelation and Worship

There is a direct relationship between revelation and worship. *Worship says back to God what He reveals.* In revelation the Lord enjoys showing us who He is and how He loves us, and in worship we enjoy Him back. His ongoing revelation is an intentional act on His part, and our ongoing worship is an intentional act on ours. This eternal dance links love full circle. As the worship chorus says, "And on and on and on and on [love] goes; it overwhelms and satisfies my soul."[25] The relationship is that simple and that profound. *I wrote this chapter and indeed this whole book to showcase this one principle.*

Revelation and the Name

The name of the Lord is also linked to worship. Many of the names of God we cherish were the fresh revelation of those who knew God before us. We see this principle span the Old and New Testaments. The Lord reminds people of His established Name or calls himself by a new Name, and people know Him more. And the converse—His people discover His character through experience and call Him by a new Name. Then they "sing to the Lord a new song, for he has done marvelous deeds" (Ps. 98:1). Meditating on the Name above all names is an encounter with God.

The Cure for "Dry" Seasons

We all have seasons of spiritual winter when the desire to worship lies dormant. At these times the Lord seems distant, and we may be disappointed or bored with our faith. Tapping back into fresh revelation about the character and ways of God cultivates new growth. If you are longing for personal revival, try some of these spirit drenching worship habits: remembering, remaining, asking, and enjoying.

Remembering

One way to awaken worship is by intentionally remembering. I simply choose a memory where the Lord revealed Himself to me— rescued me, wowed me, directed me, comforted me—then let that experience be the focus my worship right now. Many of the stories I have described in this book still draw me into fellowship with Lord. I also let my favorite scripture passages or music remind me of His past goodness, then worship in the pure awe and delight the memory brings. "I remember the days of long ago; I meditate on all your works and consider what your hands have done" (Ps. 143:5).

Responding

Another cure for dry seasons is intentionally remaining in the moment and responding to Jesus' outstretched arms. In Luke 17:11–19, Jesus is accosted by ten men who have leprosy. They beg Him for mercy and He heals them as they hurry toward their village to show themselves to the priest. Pronounced "clean," they probably went home (what a precious word) to be reunited with family and friends. But only one of the ten postponed his homecoming to return and throw himself at Jesus' feet. Jesus commended this man but was appalled at the contempt of the other nine. After all, ten had received the same healing!

We are fond of thinking, "If I'd been healed, I would've been the one who returned. The truth is that nine out of ten times we forget to respond with worship. I call this the one-in-ten rule. For every ten times the Lord reveals Himself, we respond to Him only once. The problem of worship-less-ness is not so much the inability to recognize the Lord's revelation—every leper knew he was healed—it is missing our opportunity to respond to Jesus in worship. In our fickleness we leave the time and place where the Lord has revealed Himself and forget how precious was His touch.

Sometimes we fail to respond by misdirecting our focus. For instance we have just experienced an inspiring worship service at church. We sincerely thank the pastor on our way out the door and remark to others, "Wasn't that a wonderful service?" But do we think to speak directly to God? I find that I can easily remember to thank the people who bless me, but I tend to talk *about* the Lord instead of directly *to* Him.

Another common misdirection happens when we receive an answer to prayer. We thank others for praying for us, even commenting on the quality of their prayers. It's not wrong to thank faithful family and friends, but it is wrong to ignore the Answer to their prayers.

To counteract these tendencies we simply respond to the rightful Benefactor—and do it promptly. When God speaks to me, I am trying to worship Him before I leave the encounter. For instance if I am at a retreat, I might slip outside to thank the Lord for all I've experienced on the weekend as others are preparing to leave. If I'm at church, I might stay in the sanctuary to intentionally lock eyes with the One I love. If I have the privilege of facilitating a gathering, I might use the closing prayer to say back to God what He has just revealed to us. I *try* to do these things—but fail too often. It's at home that I fail the most. A personal goal is to learn to focus on worship better in the day-to-day. I would like to be characterized by prompt, pure worship. I've even started saying or singing my worship aloud to make sure it happens. It is such joy to respond wholeheartedly and know Jesus is rightfully reverenced.

Asking

But what do we do when there is no awe-inspiring past or present revelation? We unabashedly ask the Lord to reveal Himself again! The Lord is by no means sorry when we want to know Him more, and there is always more of Him to be known. He wants us to ask Him to reveal Himself and has specifically invited us to do so. "Ask and you will receive, and your joy will be complete" (John 16:24). Next we remain at attention and promptly worship Him in the midst of His fresh revelation. Yes, He *longs* for us to ask.

Enjoying

The essence of this whole book is the prayer that must worship. It is the pinnacle of prayer. The Lord speaks, revealing marvelous things, and we know Him more—glory to glory. Then we worship, which is our reasonable service and delight. The first question of *The Westminister Shorter Catechism*[26] asks: "What is the primary purpose of man?" The answer: "Man's primary purpose is to glorify God and enjoy Him forever." The prayer that must worship—this conversation of love revealed and love returned—is the rich, full existence we were born to enjoy. We each have the honor of perceiving and responding to Love, and Love is a Person.

Going Deeper
Questions for Small Group Discussion

1. Revelation is a sudden or dawning insight into the character and ways of God through scripture, prayer, nature or experience. Take a few minutes to think back over your life. What have been your most spiritually impactful experiences? What did God reveal about His character and ways?

2. Worship is simply recognizing and responding to God's revelation or saying back to God what He reveals. What has the Lord revealed to you this year? This week? Today? What is your response?

3. How can you become more attentive to the Holy Spirit's revelation? How can you worship Him more directly and promptly?

4. Which name of God is dearest to you? Why?

5. Do you agree with the one in ten rule? How can you change the stats on this vital link in your relationship with Jesus?

6. Are you spiritually dry or bored with your Christian life? What is your plan to pursue personal revival?

The Prayer that Must Be Silent
Immersed in Love

Deep calls to deep in the roar of your waterfalls;
all your waves and breakers have swept over me.
By day the Lord directs his love, at night his song is with me
—a prayer to the God of my life.
Ps. 42:7,8

Be still, and know that I am God
Ps. 46:10.

You will remember my "birthday" stories shared in previous chapters. This testimony concerns the adventure in prayer that followed my 2008 birthday petition: "Lord, show me Your glory." I admit that in asking I had little conception of what the Lord would reveal. I only knew Moses had modeled this request in Exodus 33 when he dared ask, "Now, show me your glory" (Ex. 33:18). More exciting, Jesus asked His Father to show us His glory in John 17:24: "Father, I want those you have given me to be with me where I am, and to see my glory, the glory you have given me because you loved me before the creation of the world."

In the next months, when I sensed that the Lord was near, I tensed, wondering if this was the moment, but month after month passed and I didn't experience anything that could be called a revelation of His glory. From time to time I reminded the Lord that I was waiting by faith—not impatiently—but with anticipation. I knew by this time that some gifts take a whole year, or lifetime to give.

In the meantime a close friend had lent me a masterful treatise on prayer—Richard Foster's *Prayer: Finding the Heart's True Home.*[27] So rich were the descriptions of prayer, I could read only a few pages at a sitting, but after many months, I reached the chapter intriguingly titled "Contemplative Prayer." Here Foster described simple, silent communion with the Lord, warning that it was not prayer for the novice.

I had never experienced what he described in those pages—but I wanted to. Setting aside time to seek silence before the Lord, I began to practice to that end by opening with my typical mentally articulated words of praise or petition, and closing with a time of silence. After many weeks of awkward practice, I began to sense what Jesus described as "rivers of living water" (John 7:38). The flow of the Spirit could be described as a tender excitement, or rising joy. Lingering there in His presence, I enjoyed Him without the need to speak. The more I practiced, the easier it became to enter through silence. He is a patient and responsive Teacher.

Some months later, the Lord revealed that contemplative prayer is also a practical tool for intercession. The revelation came as I was reading through our church's emailed prayer requests and fumbling with how to phrase a decent prayer for the healing of a man I'd never met. Have you ever wrestled with prayer requests—what words to use, or how long is long enough? Not out of wisdom or compassion, but out of frustration, I entered instead into silence on his behalf.

By this time it seemed easy and natural to do so. But here was the surprise: The Holy Spirit, already in continuous intercession for this dear man and aware of all of his public and private needs, allowed me to sense the ongoing intercession for him. I did not hear any of the articulated words of the Spirit to the Father, nor did I need that information. My part was to become aware of the love of God overshadowing him until *my* love awakened, then to acquiesce to the will of the Father for his life. I rested there with the Lord for a few moments then added, "I agree with You." In this way, my prayer blended with His. Then I went on to the next part of my day in peace. I knew that the recipient of that prayer was blessed, but no more than I! This became my habit when I had no discernment about how to pray with mentally formed words.

Some weeks later, I was seated in front of the computer screen entering into silent prayer for yet another email request, when I remembered that I was looking forward to seeing the Lord's glory—oh, joy! So I asked again, "Lord, show me your glory." In that moment He surprised me with information that changed me: "*I Am* My Glory." He was smiling when He said this. With the avowal came sudden revelation. By harmonizing with the Holy Spirit through the prayer that must be silent, I was experiencing God's glory.

Consider Jesus words in John 17:22b–23a: "I have given them the glory that you gave me, that they may be one as we are one—I in them and you in me—so that they may be brought to complete unity." Suddenly I understood that the glory of the Jesus is linked to oneness with Him and oneness with each other. I felt that the Lord had placed a wrapped gift in my lap, slipped off the bow and paper, and revealed my heart's desire. What a wondrous birthday gift!

When I originally made the request, I had wondered if I would see a supernatural manifestation of the glory of God with my physical eyes, a miracle or healing, maybe even an angel. Instead Jesus had given me the gift of stepping into union with Him and seeing His glory *with my spirit,* a gift in the vein of Ephesians 3:20—immeasurably more than all I asked or imagined, according to his power that is at work within me.

Needless to say, my prayer life has significantly changed since this revelation because though I often pray in language, I do not necessarily feel the need to say or hear articulated words when I pray. I simply rest in union with the Spirit as He rests in union with me. This is the glorious communion of silent conversation.

Now that I've enjoyed the prayer that must be silent for a season, I would like to share some thoughts on its practice. Many godly authors/mentors have been my examples in this pursuit. For further study on this topic, I recommend the scripture references in this chapter and the previously mentioned Richard Foster's *Prayer: Finding the Heart's True Home*.[28] I also gained wisdom from Madame Jeanne Guyon's *Experiencing God through Prayer*,[29] and Brother Lawrence's *The Practice of the Presence of God*.[30]

Intimacy

The prayer that must be silent is one means to spiritual intimacy, or the deeper joys of fellowship with the Lord. Suspended in the mystical union of Christ and His Church, nothing is required since all is finished. "My beloved is mine and I am his" (Song 2:16). Amen.

Below are biblical phrases that may add a broader understanding of being in relationship with the Lord beyond language. I have italicized the word *glory* in the rest of this chapter to highlight the link between intimacy and the Lord's glory.

- *Standing in Grace*—"Therefore, since we have been justified through faith, we have peace with God through our Lord Jesus Christ, through whom we have gained access by faith into this grace in which we now stand. And we boast in the hope of the *glory* of God" (Rom. 5:1–2, emphasis mine).
- *The Gift of Living Water*—"Jesus answered her, "If you knew the gift of God and who it is that asks you for a drink, you would have asked him and he would have given you living water" (John 4:10). Whoever believes in me, as Scripture has said, rivers of living water will flow from within them" (John 7:38).
- *The Peace of God's Favor*—"*Glory* to God in the highest heaven, and on earth, peace to those on whom his favor rests" (Luke 2:14, emphasis mine).
- *Unity and Oneness*—"But whoever is united with the Lord is one with him in spirit" (1 Cor. 6:17). "I pray also for those who will believe in me through their message, that all of them may be one, Father, just as you are in me and I am in you. May they also be in us so that the world may believe that you have sent me. I have given them the *glory* that you gave me, that they may be one as we are one— I in them and you

in me—so that they may be brought to complete unity" (John 17:20b–23, emphasis mine).

- *Abiding (Old English) or Remaining*—"Remain in me, as I also remain in you . . . I am the vine; you are the branches. If you remain in me and I in you, you will bear much fruit; apart from me you can do nothing . . . If you remain in me and my words remain in you, ask whatever you wish, and it will be done for you. This is to my Father's *glory*, that you bear much fruit, showing yourselves to be my disciples" (John 15:4a, 5, 7–8, emphasis mine).

- *Having Done All, Stand*—"Therefore put on the full armor of God, so that when the day of evil comes, you may be able to stand your ground, and after you have done everything, to stand" (Eph. 6:13).

- *To Be Known and Know in Part*—"Now I know in part; then I shall know fully, even as I am fully known" (1 Cor. 13:12b). We know in part here on earth but are fully known at all times.

- *Fellowship with the Holy Spirit*—"May the grace of the Lord Jesus Christ, and the love of God, and the fellowship of the Holy Spirit be with you all" (2 Cor. 13:14).

- *Intimacy with God*—Song of Songs

- *Entering in*—"I am the gate; whoever enters through me will be saved. They will come in and go out, and find pasture" (John 10:9).

- *Rest, Being Instead of Doing, Sabbath*—"Therefore, since the promise of entering his rest still stands, let us be careful that none of you be found to have fallen short of it" (Heb. 4:1). "For anyone who enters God's rest also rests from their works, just as God did from his" (Heb. 4:10).

- *Beyond the Veil*—"With a loud cry, Jesus breathed his last . . . The curtain of the temple was torn in two from top to bottom. And when the centurion, who stood there in front of Jesus, saw how he died, he said, 'Surely this man was the Son of God'" (Mark 15:37–39)! "Tell me, you whom I love, where you graze your flock and where you rest your sheep at midday. Why should I be like a veiled woman beside the flocks of your friends" (Song 1:7)?

- *Yoked*—"Take my yoke upon you and learn from me, for I am gentle and humble in heart, and you will find rest for your souls" (Matt. 11:29).

Entering Silence

The goal of the prayer that must be silent is to enter the presence of the Lord and remain there as long as it pleases Him. Each of us is welcomed into the presence of God in unique ways, but there are enduring commonalities that facilitate oneness with Him. These have blessed my life:

Spiritual Hunger
Spiritual hunger could be described as an unquenched longing. We want the Lord so much it hurts. Sometimes the longing aches a little, but the longing can be terrible too—strong spiritual hunger drives us to forsake all other loves to pursue the Lord until He is found. If we do not have spiritual hunger, we can ask the Lord for it. "As the deer pants for streams of water, so my soul pants for you, my God. My soul thirsts for God, for the living God. When can I go and meet with God" (Psalm 42:1–2)?

Meditation
Meditating on the attributes and name of the Lord—His beauty, kindness, mercy, etc.—prepares our hearts for fellowship. Sincere honor and affection open the portal of His presence. As the old hymn "Blessed Assurance" states, we are "filled with His goodness, lost in His love."

Savoring Scripture
Madame Jeanne Guyon (1648–1717), a French activist for "Quietism," advises that we begin silent prayer by reading scripture slowly, thoughtfully, lingering over the rich meaning. The goal is not to memorize, study or even finish a passage, only to savor it phrase by phrase. By fastening our attention on the One who articulated the written words, we acclimate to greet Him.

Rich Music

Music takes me deep into fellowship almost immediately and keeps me there. A beautiful melody and meaningful words help discipline my mind by curving me back into prayer when my thoughts stray. I collect music that quickly ushers me into intimacy.

These are the some of the means to silent unity that God has most used in my experience. You, no doubt, are already aware of how the Lord moves you into oneness. Whatever the means, our goal is the same: intimate communion with the Jesus.

In the Silence

As we enter the prayer that must be silent the Holy Spirit may manifest as a tender, joyful stirring, or weighty, authoritative power. When He, the object of our desire, has come, the clamor of getting in tune with the Him should cease. We honor Him best by simply enjoying His fellowship. The Lord is in His holy temple [your heart and mine]; let all the earth be silent before him" (Hab. 2:20).

Jeanne Guyon offers this illustration. When we build a fire, we fan the flame to ignite the tinder, but once the flame is established, we cease our activity lest our exertion put it out. After the Lord enters our worship, no further activity is needed. The Spirit's flame burns best unhindered. When His presence subsides, we can slip back into the language of prayer, then cease again as His presence rises once more.

Resting in these moments, we find that Jesus releases us to *be* without striving to *do*. In the silence is sweet union. Some of the richest revelations of His will and wisdom come in the silent margin between spoken prayer and hurrying on.

For those who have not enjoyed this kind of fellowship but would like to, let me try to make it practical from my experience. Slipping away to a private place I often (but not often enough) kneel or lay prostrate and invite the Holy Spirit to be with me. But any quiet time, place and position work well. I may use music or scripture to help separate my mind from frenzied business.

Beginning in spoken prayer, I change to silence as the presence of the Lord enters. "Send me your light and your faithful care, let them lead me: let them bring me to your holy mountain, to the place where you dwell. Then I will go to the altar of God, to God, my joy and my delight" (Psalm 43:3–4a). There's nothing like resting in His embrace.

But I don't always enter the prayer that must be silent in so formal a manner. When my thoughts turn to Him, I can enter into communion any place or time. I describe this decision as "turning to face Him." But I must add that my disciplined prayer times fuel the informal, spontaneous prayer by giving me a quick breakthrough, meaning I enter into the prayer that must be silent more effortlessly the more I intentionally practice. "You, God, are my God, earnestly I seek you; I thirst for you, my whole being longs for you, in a dry and parched land where there is no water. I have seen you in the sanctuary and beheld your power and your *glory*. Because your love is better than life, my lips will *glorify* you . . . I cling to you; your right hand upholds me" (Psalm 63:1–3, 8, emphasis mine).

How to Intercede from Silence

Part of being one with the Lord is caring about those He loves. However, praying for others does not necessarily involve knowing the details or articulating a prayer in spoken words. By faith we can channel our intentional prayer into His ongoing intercession while resting in union with Him.

Generally, I begin silent intercession by intentionally directing my thoughts toward what I know in the natural, for instance: the name of the person, the details of a specific prayer request, or the demographics of a people group. When I know specific needs sometimes the Lord leads me to remember how I felt in similar circumstances. As I meditate and remember, my concern rises. This part of the prayer involves the exertion of my will and the perseverance to press in. As the presence of the Lord enters the prayer, I cease my work and allow His compassion to wash over and through me.

Sometimes His strong intercession brings genuine tears of grief for people I do not know. Jesus—our High Priest, and the Holy Spirit—our Intercessor (Rom. 8:26–27, Rom. 8:34, Heb. 8:1–6) express the needs to the Father; I simply cooperate with the surge of His mercy. I trust Him to know the details and He trusts me to love His people even to the point of personal sorrow. In this unity God's power is released. "Now if we are children, then we are heirs—heirs of God and co-heirs with Christ, if indeed we share in his sufferings in order that we may also share in his *glory*" (Rom. 8:17, emphasis mine). Notice here the relationship between sharing in His suffering and experiencing His glory. The Holy Spirit, who is God with us, expresses the sorrow of pain, disease, and depravity to the Father. The Father's heart through Jesus is mercy. When our hearts are broken for what breaks His, we are his true sons and daughters. Sorrow is the responsibility and glory is the lavish reward of intercessors.

How to Minister from Silence

Ministry and intercession are similar. By *ministry* I mean that part of serving others that invites them to meet with the Lord for themselves.

My friend Christine blessed me with a description about the transition between the presentation of truth (preaching, teaching, testimony) and the demonstration of it (prophecy, healing, miracles). Christine shared that as she closes the teaching portion of a service, she stops and waits before the Lord until she discerns the Spirit's compassion for those who sit before her. The direction may be towards an affliction, a longing, a need, or a specific person or group. That knowledge is held in confidence as she asks for revelation about how to speak what the Lord trusts her to know. She speaks only when the *encouragement* is revealed. Her practice is to phrase the invitation for ministry as a question that allows each person to decide how he or she would like to respond.

This advice seemed like wisdom to me, so the very next Sunday I tried it for myself. I serve on the praise team of my local church. As the worship set ended and our pastor began the morning prayer, I knelt on the platform and closed my eyes. Turning to face the Lord in the Spirit, I asked to understand His desire for the congregation seated before me and waited. Almost immediately I felt (saw) the direction of His heart. Sorrow and love were reaching out at a forty-five degree angle towards those seated to my right. With eyes closed, I waited for the pastoral prayer to end, not knowing whom the Lord's love was encompassing.

At the "amen," I opened my eyes and looked curiously to my right. The only people seated there were visitors that morning. Because they were the family members of a close friend, who was praying for their salvation, I knew that they were not yet in relationship with the Lord. He was grieving over them, reaching for them. The rest of the congregation, friends that I knew well, were already walking with the Lord.

My next impression came from Matthew18:12–13, "What do you think? If a man owns a hundred sheep, and one of them wanders away, will he not leave the ninety-nine on the hills and go to look for the one that wandered off? And if he finds it, truly I tell you, he is happier about that one sheep than about the ninety-nine that did not wander off." There happened to be about one hundred people in service that day, yet The Good Shepherd's focus was on those who were wandering. This is the characterization of our God!

Hugging the knowledge close, I wondered what to do with this inside information. Had I been in a place of authority, I may have concluded the service with a gentle altar call from the standpoint of the Good Shepherd looking for His sheep. As it was, I greeted the visitors warmly at the close of the service, watching for an opportunity to minister. Not receiving the Spirit's permission to mention what the Lord had revealed or act on it in any way, I rested in God's mercy on their behalf.

This exciting aspect of ministry is still new to me, but I am looking forward to adventures of this kind in the future.

Remaining in Love

"As the Father has loved me, so have I loved you. Now remain in my love" (John 15:9). Jesus wants us to operate in Heaven's currency—the substance and sustenance of His love. To do so, we first connect, then remain. Jesus explained life of oneness with Him in this way, "No branch can bear fruit by itself; it must remain in the vine. Neither can you bear fruit unless you remain in me. I am the vine; you are the branches. If you remain in me and I in you, you will bear much fruit; apart from me you can do nothing" (John 15:4b–5).

The prayer that must be silent helps us practice entering and remaining in the God. It trains us to reference our relationship with

Him from intimacy. Jesus promises that a connected life will bear much fruit. The end of the matter is not only the joy and blessing we receive from union with Jesus, but the fruitfulness of His ever-reaching love flowing through us into our realm of influence. In this way we are immersed to overflowing in Love, and Love is a Person.

Going Deeper
Questions for Small Group Discussion

1. How do you define the glory of God?

2. How do you best pray for the needs of others—especially those you do not know?

3. With which of the biblical descriptions of spiritual intimacy do you most identify? Which do you most want/need to experience in your prayer life?

4. There are many ways to intimately connect with God. How do you enter His presence?

5. Have you ever interceded for others or ministered from silence? Describe that experience.

The Prayer That Must Leave A Legacy
Bequeathing Love

Then we your people, the sheep of your pasture, will praise you forever;
from generation to generation we will proclaim your praise.

Ps. 79:13

One of my favorite books is C.S. Lewis's *The Last Battle*,[31] the final installment in *The Chronicles of Narnia*. If you have not read the series, let me add my recommendation to the myriad of other voices that have done so and encourage you to make this a delightful personal or family read soon.

In this story we step at last into Aslan's Country (heaven), where we will never be parted from Aslan (the Lord) or those we love again. A fascinating aspect of that beloved place is that the "inside is bigger than the outside." "Further up and further in" brings us into a walled garden, which is bigger than the whole world outside the enclosure.

A life of relational prayer is like that walled garden, an infinite, supernatural world within a limited, natural one. As our conversations in prayer reveal our Father, His presence, His perspective, His power transforms the dialog into limitlessness. As I shared in the introduction, prayer is the ultimate adventure, the launching place to all destinations.

In the previous chapters we have tapped nine avenues of limitlessness prayer:

- When we must know, the Lord answers our specific questions in specific ways. He leads us in paths of righteousness for His Name's sake.
- When the answer we seek tarries, and we must wait, the Lord sustains us in the interim and works all things together for our good. *He* is worth hoping and waiting for.
- When we face a battle that we must win, each of us is responsible to stand in God our Savior. That doesn't mean that everything will turn out the way we want—but it does mean the Lord is mighty to save.
- When the Lord speaks, we must write what He reveals. Our continuing conversation with Jesus is unique and valuable. A life of prayer includes leaving influential clues about our walk with God.
- When our painful emotions reveal embedded lies, only the Lord of Truth can set us free. He is our healing and peace.
- When we must let go of what we love, Jesus both understands and values our sacrifice. We can trust Him to hold us as we release the dearest parts of who we are and those we love back to Him.
- When God reveals His character and ways, we must worship. We were created to enjoy the Lord forever.
- When entering the on-going intercession of the Holy Spirit, we must be silent and rest in His embrace. In the silence is intimacy.

The prayer that must leave a legacy is the cumulative *influence* of all these conversations with God. Like a seed that holds the potential for a hundred more, so our conversations with the Lord are fruitful beyond our understanding. They bear fruit in other places and times, more than we think or imagine. The prayer that must leave a legacy is a gift for people we may not know until heaven, a most wise and intentional investment. Friend, we can little fathom what God has planned for those who love Him. In the prayer that must leave a legacy we bequeath Love, and Love is a Person.

A Final Prayer

Jesus,

You are Holy and beautiful. We know You a little—but we unabashedly ask to know You more. Speak to us and teach us to respond to You. Emphatically yes!

Give each of us the courage to accept for ourselves Your redeeming work through Jesus, then surprise us with a relationship that exceeds all we've asked or imagined. May we long for more of Your presence and stay in tune with the movement of Your Spirit. Teach us to hunger and thirst for You—especially a deeper relationship with Jesus as friend.

When we feel alone, abandoned, or neglected, teach us to trust again. As we rest in Your embrace heal our deepest hurts. We are willing come home to our Father's loving arms.

We want to be so satisfied by Your love that we bubble over into sacrificial love for others. Channel Your empathy and mercy through our yielded lives. We want to love best and influence most at home, but urge us to pray and influence way beyond ourselves. May our pending prayers cause other places and generations to rejoice.

Today we formally entrust family members that we will not meet until heaven into Your care. Lead them into intimate union with You. Give wisdom to our children and children's children as they establish their homes. May their marriages represent the union of Christ and His Church. Teach them to parent like You. Build them into Your Church that they may move as one body under one Lord. Use their witness to glorify Your name and make them influential to who follow their example. May their ministry exceed ours.

Protect us from our enemy. In due season present us faultless before Your throne with great joy. We trust You to do all this and wait in expectation to see Your Kingdom advance through us. Give us the power to finish strong.

We trust in Your goodness.

In Jesus name, Amen.

His Reply to Me

Speak to Me—I love your voice. I am performing My goodness and will be faithful to answer your prayers. Thank you for loving My people.

Going Deeper
Questions for Small Group Discussion

1. Are you the beneficiary of the prayers of those who lived before you? Who are the prayer warriors in your family line and among your mentors? What were their specific prayers? What is the lasting influence of their lives?

2. If all your prayers were answered in a single moment, what would change in this generation? What would change in the generations to come?

3. Write a specific prayer for your children's generation, your grandchildren's generation, and your great-grandchildren's generation. Place your written prayers where they will be cherished and preserved.

Who is God?
Appendix One

God is a Spirit, Whose being, wisdom, power, holiness, justice, goodness, and truth are infinite, eternal, and unchangeable. There is only one God. He is living and true. There are three persons in the one God: the Father, the Son and the Holy Spirit. These three are one God, the same in substance and equal in power and glory.

The Westminister Shorter Catechism[32]

The Father Heart of God

Beyond Scripture my favorite description of the Father has already been written so I won't add my comments here. To understand more about God, our Father, I recommend these excellent resources: Jack Winter's teachings on "The Father Heart of God,"[33] and *The Father Heart of God: Experiencing the Depths of His Love for You,* by Floyd McClung.[34] Richard and I heard these teachings firsthand serving in YWAM, Amsterdam in 1983 and have treasured the wisdom they contain.

Jesus, the One and Only

There is no one like Jesus. He brings salvation, healing, and peace. His presence changes people and circumstances. How does He transform the whole world and everyone in it? Here is a brief glimpse of who He is.

Jesus Reveals the Father

Jesus is the beloved of the Father. In Him the Father is well pleased (Matt. 3:17). God made Himself visible in His Son. Clothed in obedience, Jesus came to do the exact will of His Father and manifest His accurate image to us (John 8:28). All of the actions and emotions, grace and truth, power and restraint of the Father were demonstrated in the life of His only Son. He is the essence of His Father, God made flesh (John 1:14, Matt. 1:18–23). When Philip, one of the twelve, asked Jesus to show him the Father, Jesus answered, "Don't you know me, Philip, even after I have been among you such a long time? Anyone who has seen me has seen the Father. How can you say, 'Show us the Father'" (John 14:9)? Indeed the Great I Am is made known.

Jesus is the Center

Jesus is the author and culmination of creation, the Word (Col. 1:15–17, John 1:1–3), meaning the First Source of all things. As the focal point of Scripture, the Old Testament saints wait in anticipation for His appearing; and the New Testament saints documents His earthly life and explain why His life alone transforms every other life.

In the Gospels Jesus demonstrated love in action because He *is* love. He preached the truth with authority because He *is* Truth. He performed miraculous signs because He *is* Creator. His act of redemption was powerful because He *is* the power of God unto salvation.

Jesus is Eternal Life

There is only one God and only one way to know Him. Only Jesus, His Son (Acts 4:12) leads us into an unending relationship with the Father. The way to eternal life is narrow, but clearly marked, so that we are without excuse (Rom.1:20). Jesus is the beginning of the beginning, the end of all things, and the Eternal One.

Jesus is Love

Love is defined by Jesus' sacrificial life. The Father gave His Son, and the Son lay down His life for all of us. Love culminated in supreme mercy and justice, as Jesus was nailed to a cross to die, willingly laying down his life for the sins of the whole world. Rising from the grave, He defeated death for all time (John 3:16). He did that even while we were still sinners (Rom. 5:8). We know by His example that there is no love without sacrifice.

Those who surrender their lives to Jesus, accepting his gift of forgiveness of sin and eternal life in Heaven (Luke 1:77, John 3:16), take up their own "cross" and follow Him (Matt. 16:24) to a life of obedience (John 14:15, James 1:22), humility (Mark 10:21, 1 Pet. 5:6) and sacrifice (Matt. 10:39, Mark 10:29–31).

Jesus is Not . . .

Jesus is not merely a good man. He is God. He is not simply a prophet. He is the one who writes and fulfills all prophecy. He is not one of many wise teachers; He is the author of all wisdom, and absolute Truth is based on His character. He will never share His glory with another.

Jesus is . . .

- Messiah (John 1:41)
- Christ, the Anointed One (Matt. 1:16)
- Teacher (Matt. 8:19)
- Savior (Matt. 1:21)
- The way, truth and life (John 14:6)
- Lamb of God (John 1:36)
- Son of God (Mark 1:1)
- Son of Man (Luke 19:20)
- Master (Luke 5:5)
- The Good Shepherd (John 10:11)
- Lion of the Tribe of Judah (Rev. 5:5)
- Morning Star (Rev. 22:16)
- King of Kings and Lord of Lords (Rev. 17:14)

Holy Spirit, Our Confidant and Power

Holy Spirit is eternally God. His activity is seen throughout the scriptures, and He indwells every person who will invite Him in. The Spirit's tender but powerful movement is the evidence that God is with us.

Holy Spirit is the Power of God

The scriptures open with the activity and emotion of the Spirit of God, brooding over the waters in Genesis 1:2. He anoints the Old and New Testament patriarchs, prophets, judges, kings, apostles, evangelists, pastors, and teachers: the Spirit is God's power (Luke 1:35, Luke 4:14, Acts 1:8). Every act of God in the Scriptures is produced by the power of Holy Spirit.

The Spirit is the Third Person of the Godhead

At Jesus' earthly conception, Holy Spirit overshadowed Mary (Luke 1:35). He is therefore the Spirit of our Heavenly Father (Jn. 14:26). Simultaneously, he is the Spirit of Jesus (Phil. 1:19). He brings forth the truth of Jesus' words and His glory (John 16:13 -15). As the third person of the Trinity (Matt. 28:19), He is unique, yet one with the Father and the Son (John 14:10–11, 15–17).

The voice of the Father and the presence of the Spirit simultaneously verified Jesus' earthly ministry at His baptism (Mark 1:10–11).

Holy Spirit is Indwelling God

Jesus explained that it would be to our advantage that He depart and send His Spirit to indwell us (John 16:5–7), be our guide (Matt. 4:1, John 16:13), wisdom (Isa. 11:2, Acts 6:10, Eph. 1:17), and power (Acts 1:7–8). On the day of Pentecost, Holy Spirit was given to the Church so that Jesus could be with each of us at all times. He is our teacher, reminding us of everything Jesus said (John 14:26).

Jesus is now in Heaven. He is not physically with us as when He lived with His first disciples, but He assured us that we would never be alone by giving us His Spirit.

In the moment of "The Exchange," our salvation decision, Holy Spirit is given as the down payment and proof that we are sons and daughters of God (Eph. 1:13–14). Our bodies become His Holy Temple (1 Cor. 6:19). He convicts our sin and encourages us. He baptizes and fills us. He brings His powerful gifts and produces fruit in keeping with His character in the lives of believers (Ex. 31:3; Deut. 24:9; Matt. 3:11; Luke 1:41; Acts 1:5, 4:31, 8:16, 9:31; Rom. 12:4–8; 1 Cor. 2:12, 12:1–13; Gal. 5:22–25).

Holy Spirit is Our Unity

Holy Spirit is our intercessor, relaying to the Father what we long to express (Rom. 8:26). Given to be our Advocate (John 14:16, 26), and Sanctifier (2 Thess. 2:13, 1 Pet 1:2), He builds the Church up into the Head, who is Christ, until we all come to maturity and unity (Eph. 4:3).

One day soon Jesus will return and gather His Church to Heaven (Acts 1:6–11). As we wait, Holy Spirit unifies the whole Church in all generations and places. His voice blends with ours to urgently call for Jesus' return (Rev. 22:17a).

Holy Spirit's Name

Jesus addressed Holy Spirit as a person—*Him,* not *it* (John 14:15–17). Holy Spirit is not to be diminished or grieved. Jesus sternly warned the Pharisees that they must not speak against Holy Spirit (Matt. 12:32), and Paul warned the early Church not to grieve Him (Eph. 4:30).

Other names for Holy Spirit are: Counselor, breath of Heaven, Spirit of Glory, Spirit of truth, Spirit of wisdom and understanding, Comforter, the gift, the voice of the Lord, the power of God. The acts of Holy Spirit are found throughout the scriptures, but in particular John 14 and 16, the book of Acts, and Paul's letters.

Erin's Second Song
Appendix Two

The Lord intentionally comforts us as we release the dearest parts of ourselves and those we love into His waiting arms. This is the story of how He comforted me concerning Erin White's departure to Heaven.

The Wednesday before Erin's death on Sunday, Richard and I received a call from Linda (her mother). Erin had weakened so much in a week's time that she was sure the end was near. She encouraged us to visit soon. We were stunned. Hadn't she just been at church on Sunday? In sorrow I asked the Holy Spirit for the words to form a prayer. For all these months we had prayed for a complete healing, but I didn't sense I was to pray for healing now. In my confusion, the Holy Spirit came beside me and helped me pray the prayer that must let go.

"Lord, may Erin's death be in a peaceful sleep."

I have read many accounts of near death experiences. In those testimonies some saints are greeted in heaven by a close relative. An angel escorts others. Still others testify—oh, blessed thought—that Jesus Himself comes to meet them. So, I added, "Please come to meet her Yourself, Jesus, so that Yours is the first face Erin sees. And when she sees You, let there be some memorable indication so that Linda and Charlie will always have that knowledge to comfort them."

Then I added one last specific request. "May I have the honor of seeing her entrance into Heaven from earth's side?" Even as I made this request I felt selfish, but deep in my heart I wanted to be at her bedside to say goodbye and know she was with Jesus.

I did visit—minutes after Erin's University of Tulsa professors presented her diploma on Friday evening. Whenever I thought of Erin in the next two days, I prayed and of course, grieved.

On Monday morning, April 21, the phone rang at 6:30 a.m. When I heard our dear friend, Oman Guthrie's greeting, I knew Erin had died.

My first question was, "Is she gone?"

"Yes, she died last night about 11:15."

Remembering my prayer, I had to ask, "What was her death like?"

He answered with such tenderness, "It was just like heaven."

Later I learned that as praise choruses filled the room, she peacefully died in her sleep. Minutes later Charlie and Linda and a few friends knelt around her bed. They held Erin's hands, thanked the Father for her life, and committed her to Him. How beautiful! Surrounded by those who loved her and sleeping peacefully in her own praise-filled room, the Lord had taken Erin to her new home. Those who witnessed her departure testified that the presence of God had been tangible and had comforted them. I could not have been more thankful. No, *I* had not been there, but that had been the selfish part of my prayer after all. Despite the pain the Lord had been faithful to us all. I did not know then that Jesus would answer every word of my prayer in His own time. The Lord often guides the words of our prayers because He is about to answer them in surprising ways.

Several evenings later, as I drove home from a late-night meeting, I happened to switch on the tape deck. A song began on the first note as if on cue. I listened in shocked disbelief, then mounting awe, as the song became a prophetic revelation in Erin's own words, it seemed. She was relating to me her last moments here on earth and her first thoughts of Heaven. As the song continued, I awakened with her after sleeping and felt with her the strangeness of being away from home, yet completely at home. I struggled with her as she longed to go back, yet did not want to leave. Then I heard her describe the face of Jesus . . .

Pulling into the carport at home, I sat and re-listened. The time was a little after 11 p.m., about the same time she had died five nights before.

As the song ended for the second time—suddenly—the memory of my specific prayer came back to me. I had longed to be with Erin at the end of her life and see with my own eyes her safe passage to Heaven. I had asked Jesus to meet her in person. I had asked that Charlie and Linda would have an outward sign that He had personally come to welcome Erin on the other side. Only He knew what I had prayed. He alone could have revealed this information.

I thought morning would never come so that I could call the Whites and reverently share "Erin's Second Song."

I Saw the Lord, "Erin's Second Song"
Dallas Holm, 1996

The place was white as snow and pure as finest gold.
It had the look of new; it had the look of old.
I felt like I was home, but felt so far away;
In fear I fought to leave, but felt the urge to stay.

Then a silence fell like none I'd ever known.
I stood among the millions, I stood there all alone.
His face was like the sun, His eyes were like the sea,
His voice was like the thunder rolling through eternity.

Chorus
And I saw the Lord
He was high and lifted up and rightfully adored
And I saw the Lord—
And he saw me. El Roi

Then from sleep awakened, I looked into the night,
The darkness overtaken by a bright and shining light.
Oh, I couldn't understand it, and I couldn't reason how,
Then my eyes beheld Him, I wasn't dreaming now!

Chorus

Notes

[1] Catherine Marshall, *Beyond Our Selves* (Grand Rapids, MI: Chosen Books, 2001, first published 1961).

[2] Sandra Strange, *Be Aglow and Burning with the Spirit* (Amazon Createspace, 2015).

[3] Rebecca Springer, *Within Heaven's Gates* (New Kinsington, PA: Whitaker House, 1984).

[4] Benny Hinn, *Good Morning, Holy Spirit* (Nashville, TN: Thomas Nelson Publishers, 1997).

[5] "Praise to the Lord, the Almighty." Text: Joachim Neander (1680); Music: Erneuerten Gesangbuch; Translater: Catherine Winkworth (1863); Tune: Lobe Den Herren.

[6] Henry T. Blackaby and Claude V. King, *Experiencing God, Knowing and Doing the Will of God* (Nashville, TN: Lifeway, 1990).

[7] J. S. Bach, "Jesu, Joy of Man's Desiring," Herz und Mund und Tat und Leben, BWV 147 (1716 and 1723), translated by poet laureate Robert Bridges (late 1800's).

[8] C. S. Lewis, *Prince Caspian*, *The Chronicles of Narnia* (New York, NY: HarperCollins Publishers, 1979).

[9] James W. and Michal Ann Goll, *Dream Language* (Shippensburg, PA: Destiny Image Publishers, Inc., 2006).

[10] Del Tackett, *The Truth Project*, Christian Worldview Small Group Curriculum (Colorado Springs, CO: Focus on the Family, 2007).

[11] Blackaby and King, *Experiencing God*.

[12] Jamie Lash, *A Kiss A Day: 77 Days in the Love of God from the Song of Songs* (Hagerstown, MD: Ebed Publications, 2000).

[13] Corrie ten Boom quote 10/1946, Pam Rosewell Moore, *Life Lessons from the Hiding Place* (Grand Rapids, MI: Chosen Books, 2005), 121.

[14] Dr. Michael Wells, "Marriage Essentials," Center for Family Ministries Midwinter Couple's Retreat: Glen Erie Conference Center, Colorado Springs, CO, Feb. 4–6, 2000.

[15] Edith Schaeffer, Lecture titled "Job, Pt. 2," L'Abri Fellowship Library http://www.labri-ideas-library.org/store/22.3%20Job%20Part%202%20-%20Whether%20We%20Live%20in%20a%20Moral%20or%20Amoral%20Universe%20-%20Francis%20Schaeffer.mp3 (accessed Jan. 23, 2014).

[16] Darren Wilson, *Furious Love, This Time Love Fights Back* (Wanderlust Productions, edited by Darren Wilson and Braden Heckman, 2010), Website furiouslove.com.

[17] C. S. Lewis, *The Chronicles of Narnia, Prince Caspian* (Produced by Walden Media and Walt Disney Pictures, directed by Andrew Adamson, 2008).

[18] Jan Sjoerd Pasterkamp, Interview with Daren Wilson, *Furious Love*.

[19] Noah Webster, *American Dictionary of the English Language*, 1828.

[20] John Venturella, "Erin's Song," CD titled "In His Care," written and produced by John Venturella, 1996, performed by Debra Ramirez (Profile Press Inc., 1997).

[21] Catherine Marshall, *Beyond Our Selves*.

[22] Bill Gothard, *Institute in Basic Life Principles Seminar,* http://iblp.org for seminar schedule.

[23] Jan Karon, *At Home in Mitford* (New York, NY: Penguin Books, 1996).

[24] Judson Cornwall, *Worship as Jesus Taught It* (Tulsa, OK: Victory House Publishers, 1987).

[25] "One Thing Remains," CD titled "Come Away," written by Brian Johnson, Jeremy Riddle, Christa Black, performed by Jesus Culture (Published by Lyrics Music Services, Inc., 2010).

[26] Douglas Kelly and Philip Rollinson, *The Westminister Shorter Catechism in Modern English* (Phillipsburg, New Jersey: Presbyterian and Reformed Publishing Company, 1986).

[27] Richard Foster, *Prayer: Finding the Heart's True Home* (New York, NY: HarperCollins Publishers, 1992).

[28] Ibid.

[29] Madame Jeanne Guyon, *Experiencing God through Prayer* (Gainsville, FL: Bridge-Logos, 2004).

[30] Brother Lawrence, *The Practice of the Presence of God* (New Kinsington, PA, Whitaker House, 1982, first published 1691).

[31] C.S. Lewis, *The Last Battle, The Chronicles of Narnia* (New York, NY: HarperCollins Publishers, 1979).

[32] Kelly and Rollinson, *The Westminister Shorter Catechism in Modern English.*

[33] Jack Winter teachings on "The Father Heart of God," https://www.youtube.com/watch?v=Smie0a5gdVM (assessed March 2017).
Jack Winter, *The Homecoming: Unconditional Love: Finding Your Place in the Father's Heart* (YWAM Publishing, 1997).

[34] *The Father Heart of God: Experiencing the Depths of His Love for You,* by Floyd McClung (Eugene, OR: Harvest House Publishers, 1985).

About the Author

Susan teaches elementary and junior high writing at Christian Education Alliance in Tulsa.

Website
missioninjoy.me

Blog
jointjournal.me.

Various Articles
http://christianfamilyheritage.org/blog/

The Ekhoffs have seven children: Benjamin; Hannah, her husband David and their daughter Eleanor; Lydia; Mary and her husband Nathan; Samuel; Julia; and John. Susan and Richard attend LifeChurch, South Tulsa. They make their home in Tulsa, OK.

Other Books by Susan Ekhoff

The Lamp, Be Aglow and Burning with the Spirit, by Sandra Strange with Susan Ekhoff
Adopted, by Gloria Fuller with Susan Ekhoff, due for publish early 2018

54681310R00117

Made in the USA
San Bernardino, CA
22 October 2017